Online Hate and Harmful Content

In times of ever-increasing changes in technology and online socio-cultural trends, there is a constant and pressing need for updated knowledge. This book provides the most up-to-date study of online hate speech and harms associated with the Internet. By presenting ground-breaking comparative research and introducing new concepts such as Identity Bubble Reinforcement, it breaks new ground both empirically and theoretically.

Sveinung Sandberg, *Professor, University of Oslo*

Over the past few decades, various types of hate material have caused increasing concern. Today, the scope of hate is wider than ever, as easy and often-anonymous access to an enormous amount of online content has opened the Internet up to both use and abuse. By providing possibilities for inexpensive and instantaneous access without ties to geographic location or a user identification system, the Internet has permitted hate groups and individuals espousing hate to transmit their ideas to a worldwide audience.

Online Hate and Harmful Content focuses on the role of potentially harmful online content, particularly among young people. This focus is explored through two approaches: first, the commonality of online hate through cross-national survey statistics. This includes a discussion of the various implications of online hate for young people in terms of, for example, subjective wellbeing, trust, self-image and social relationships. Second, the book examines theoretical frameworks from the fields of sociology, social psychology and criminology that are useful for understanding online behaviour and online victimisation. Limitations of past theory are assessed and complemented with a novel theoretical model linking past work to the online environment as it exists today.

An important and timely volume in this ever-changing digital age, this book is suitable for graduates and undergraduates interested in the fields of Internet and new media studies, social psychology and criminology. The analyses and findings of the book are also particularly relevant to practitioners and policymakers working in the areas of Internet regulation, crime prevention, child protection and social work/youth work.

Teo Keipi is a post-doctoral researcher in Economic Sociology at the University of Turku, Finland.

Matti Näsi is a post-doctoral researcher at the Institute of Criminology and Legal Policy at the University of Helsinki, Finland.

Atte Oksanen is professor of Social Psychology at the University of Tampere, Finland.

Pekka Räsänen is professor of Economic Sociology at the University of Turku, Finland.

Routledge Advances in Sociology

For a full list of titles in this series, please visit www.routledge.com/series/SE0511

Online Hate and Harmful Content

Cross-national perspectives

Teo Keipi, Matti Näsi, Atte Oksanen and Pekka Räsänen

Routledge
Taylor & Francis Group

LONDON AND NEW YORK

First published 2017
by Routledge
2 Park Square, Milton Park, Abingdon, Oxon OX14 4RN

and by Routledge
711 Third Avenue, New York, NY 10017

Routledge is an imprint of the Taylor & Francis Group, an informa business

© 2017 Teo Keipi, Matti Näsi, Atte Oksanen and Pekka Räsänen

The right of Teo Keipi, Matti Näsi, Atte Oksanen and Pekka Räsänen to
be identified as authors of this work has been asserted by them in
accordance with sections 77 and 78 of the Copyright, Designs and Patents
Act 1988.

British Library Cataloguing in Publication Data
A catalogue record for this book is available from the British Library

Library of Congress Cataloging in Publication Data
A catalog record for this book has been requested

ISBN: 978-1-138-64506-6 (hbk)
ISBN: 978-1-315-62837-0 (ebk)

Typeset in Times New Roman
by Wearset Ltd, Boldon, Tyne and Wear

Contents

Illustrations

Figures

Tables

About the authors

Teo Keipi, Doctor of Social Sciences, is a postdoctoral researcher in Economic Sociology at the University of Turku, Finland. His research interests include identity, anonymity and Internet use with a current emphasis on the effects of harmful online content on young people.

Matti Näsi, Doctor of Social Sciences, is a postdoctoral researcher at the Institute of Criminology and Legal Policy at the University of Helsinki, Finland. His research focuses on the impacts of information and communication technologies on society and social life, with a current emphasis on the implications of harmful online content.

Atte Oksanen, Doctor of Social Sciences, is a professor of Social Psychology at the University of Tampere, Finland. His research focuses on emerging technologies and social interaction. He has published in a variety of areas including youth studies, drug and alcohol research and criminology.

Pekka Räsänen, Doctor of Social Sciences, is professor of Economic Sociology at the University of Turku, Finland. He has studied a variety of topics connected with social inequalities, mass violence, digital culture and consumer behaviour. His current research focuses on interrelationships between online and offline behaviour.

Acknowledgements

We would like to thank the Kone Foundation for funding the project, Hate Communities: A Cross-National Comparison, from 2013 to 2016. In addition, we would like to acknowledge both the Kone Foundation and the Alli Paasikivi Foundation for additional grants.

Numerous people have made our project successful, which paved the way for this book: James Hawdon, Frank Robertz, Vili Lehdonvirta, Emma Holkeri, Markus Kaakinen, Jaana Minkkinen, Anu Sirola, Tuuli Turja, Mira Stenhammar, Tuuli Ronkainen, Janna Oksanen, Jukka Sivonen. Thank you all.

1 Evolving social media

1.1 Introduction

"Can you kill yourself already?"
"Fuckin ugly ass hoe."
"Nobody even cares about you."

On 9 December 2012 16-year-old Jessica Laney was found hanged in her home in Hudson, Florida. For months prior to her suicide, Jessica had been the target of extensive cyberbullying through the popular online social media site ASKfm. Her story is devastating on its own, yet even more unnerving is that the experiences of Jessica Laney are not unlike those of Amanda Todd, Ryan Halligan, David Molak and many others. Each of these young people was bullied extensively on the Internet, eventually taking extreme measures to finally escape their tormentors. The Internet continues to foster countless similarly vile interactions and outcomes, be it through social media platforms, online discussion forums, comment sections of local news sites, or even personal email. Hate has taken up residence in the online space on a global scale.

Although the general consensus tends to stress the benefits of the Internet in the sense of its provision of a platform for free expression of opinions and convenient interaction, recent years have increasingly brought into view the darker aspects of the online world. These include various forms of negative behaviour involving cyberbullying, harassment, stalking, slander, manipulation of personal information and fraud. Information and communication technologies (ICTs) have helped terrorists and other criminal actors communicate and reinforce their activities while also manipulating sentiments with increasing effectiveness. Often, even extreme threats are communicated via mainstream channels such as Facebook or YouTube. In addition, the Internet is home to potentially disturbing and harmful content such as torture or snuff videos showing the actual deaths of people. It is also clear that certain material can be more harmful for some users and less so for others. In the discussion of potential harm, the primary focus of concern is, understandably, on children, teenagers and young adults.

This book consequently focuses on the darker aspects of the Internet through the lens of youth and young adults in particular. It does so by paying particular attention to the core force of harm in today's online society, namely the communication of hate. Online hate (i.e. cyberhate), as a global phenomenon, specifically targets either individuals or groups of people. Notably, it is not a specific exception to the rules of interaction but rather is rooted in mainstream experience. Vile and hateful online interaction is seemingly becoming the new norm even in the most socio-economically advanced Western societies. It takes many forms, often masking itself as rational opinion or justified expression. Hate, as it exists today, is of course nothing new. What is new, however, is the extent to which online tools allow global dissemination of content and ease of access to targets, and make it difficult to mitigate or prevent negative experience among users which spend a great deal of time navigating in that environment.

The modern tools afforded by these technological developments have become central to the ways in which we communicate, explore and connect to the world. Immediate access to global news, friends, interests, new contacts and modes of expression has become an assumed part of life for owners of enabling mobile phones. It could be argued that being online has become a mundane aspect of life in most Western societies, where constant connectivity is the norm. We tend not to be awestruck by the incredible capabilities afforded to us by technology in the way that someone new to this array of enhancing tools would be. Today, information, communication and entertainment are all activities that can be found in a single device not much bigger than the palm of your hand. Smartphones are, however, only a small element of a larger entity of different ICTs. Computers, laptops, mobile phones and tablet computers have all been developed to provide easy access to the online space. Furthermore, the online space itself has taken a constantly growing role in the daily life of most Western societies, even to the extent that these are referred to as a homogenous body of information societies.

Although the expanding role of the different ICTs seems relatively rapid, large-scale evolution of the new information societies began in the aftermath of their transformation into post-industrial societies (Bell, 1973). This transition took an even steeper turn roughly two decades ago, and today almost half of the world's population is able to "log in". This technologisation of Western society has introduced great changes in all aspects of everyday life. For many, working is no longer tied to a specific time or location, as one's office can be set up almost anywhere. Furthermore, leisure is increasingly spent in front of a screen, whether to read the news, watch a movie, or connect with friends. Due to the impact that different ICTs have had on both work and leisure, they have become central management tools for many of the components of everyday life. However, and to put things into a bit more perspective, computers and mobile devices are not the first, or even the biggest, wave of technological change that has hit Western homes and working life. Television, and particularly the various other electronic home appliances that were introduced to the mass market in the 1940s and 1950s, revolutionised much of society and how it would be operationalised from then onwards (Bittman, Rice & Wajcman, 2004; Cowan, 1976). However, what the Internet as a connecting mechanism has done is redraw the boundaries of communication, information and entertainment in a global context, a change unlike any other thus far.

Early computers and the predecessors of the Internet, such as ARPANET, were constructed for the purpose of helping to process and distribute information among the scientific community. Like many things originally intended for limited use, computers and the Internet eventually became an integral part of the modern-day household. The significance of these technologies at the societal level is linked to the development of a new way of conceptualising context, namely through the information society framework (e.g. Castells & Himanen, 2002) or network society (van Dijk, 2012). The information, or network, society is a concept introduced for the purposes of better understanding the growing role of new technologies within the societal context, and is a multifaceted phenomenon which has inspired a number of books. For the sake of a more focused approach, we will not delve into the theoretical discussion of the specifics of what constitutes an information society. Rather, we will focus on a few of the central elements that are associated with these societies. In particular, we are concerned with the dynamics of the darker aspects of the online society here.

In Chapters 2 and 3 we address some key theoretical tools and integrate both criminological and social psychological theories on computer-mediated behaviour. Criminologists have shown factors associated with criminal victimisation involving risk environments (e.g. Pratt, Holtfreter & Reisig, 2010; Reyns, 2013), and social psychologists have underlined the significant overlap between identity group behaviour and conditions favouring anonymity of some kind (e.g. Spears, Postmes, Lea & Wolbert, 2002). These perspectives help us to understand the behaviours of content creators and consumers, and the social dynamics at play in the online environment in terms of risk and victimisation. Chapters 4, 5 and 6 focus on the rising presence of online hate in the cross-cultural context and show empirical findings regarding exposure and impacts of online hate and harmful content among young people. In Chapter 7 we go beyond empirical observations by introducing what we call the Identity Bubble Reinforcement model, or IBR model, in order to more fully understand risky behaviour and reinforcing phenomena. Finally, in Chapter 8 we link the book's main themes together and assess implications for the future.

In order to provide a better understanding of some of the main aims of this book, we endeavour to answer the following key questions:

- What is online hate, what forms does it take, and what are the implications of exposure?
- How prevalent is exposure to hate material among young people cross-nationally and does exposure vary by nation?
- Which components of past theory can be leveraged to improve understanding of hate in the current online environment?
- How do risk factors, social identity dynamics and the mechanisms of the modern online environment relate to exposure to hate?
- How might the risk of online exposure to hate shape the future of Internet use?

The following chapters therefore aim to provide answers to these question by utilising past theoretical frameworks and recent research literature while also offering empirical interpretations based on unique cross-national survey data collected in the UK, the US, Germany and Finland. The interpretations based on our findings provide us with new possibilities for understanding the changing computer-mediated landscape in which young people of today spend an increasing proportion of daily life. We can, through our data, detect the current characteristics of exposure to hate within countries, while also mapping out common denominators in terms of hate material cross-nationally. However, before delving into the dark side of the Internet, this chapter takes a few steps back to better contextualise how we, as modern Western societies immersed in new technology, arrived where we are today. Through this, we hope to clarify some of the core elements of the present-day information society and what they were built on. In particular, we provide a brief overview of the evolving roles of social media in the rising culture of risk.

1.2 From new media to social media

"New media" is perhaps the most common and popular term associated with the distinction between old and traditional media that has resulted from the emergence of new electronic technologies. According to Livingstone (1999), the term "new media" was first coined in reference to advances in home entertainment, such as video cassette recorders (VCRs), computer games or satellite television. However, today, the common understanding of what constitutes new media has taken a slightly more evolved form. New media not only relates to the digitalisation of traditional media, such as newspapers and television (Lawson-Borders, 2003; Lievrouw, 2004), but also includes various aspects of digitised interaction, thus combining the central elements that make up the present-day technological landscape (see also van Dijk, 2012).

Perhaps the most distinctive feature of new media is their interactive nature. These interactive functions are usually referred to as *social media*. Here, we treat social media as a distinct extension of the new media phenomenon, as they have developed to the point of being a global environment combining both technology and interaction on a new scale. So what do we mean by social media? Our definition requires a bit of background on the evolution of the Internet. We argue that social media are largely an end result of the transformation from what is referred to as the Web 1.0 society into the Web 2.0 society. From a practical perspective, this was really a transformation of behaviour. That is, users were previously far more passive consumers of all aspects of online content. This was in large part due to the fact that only relatively few individuals had the capability, tools and therefore means to produce content online. These few individuals were commonly known as webmasters. As a result, much online interaction operated like a one-way street, with a unidirectional flow of information to the consumer.

With the transformation to a Web 2.0 society, a new highway was constructed. Here, content began travelling in both directions, as formerly passive users were able to become increasingly active content producers. This resulted in technological advances in both online platforms and the tools used to access the Internet. In other words, technology had become affordable, simple and accessible enough to be conveniently usable by the masses, enabling a more active role. This, in turn, meant that control over what is produced online left the hands of the few and became the property of all users. This is not to say that self-expression in the online context did not exist before Web 2.0. It did, as a number of different online discussion boards were in operation in the early 1990s. What changed, however, was the ability to produce individualised content accessible by other users in a more structured and, most importantly, global platform with the aid of user-friendly technology. As such, social media involve platforms for expression and interaction where users are able to create content and manage social networks, with Web 2.0 being closely associated with the emergence of different social media services. MySpace was among the first global social networking services to be at the front line of the transformation from passive consumption to active content production. As O'Reilly (2005) has expounded, Web 2.0 was not so much a technological upgrade from Web 1.0, but rather a transformation of how the Internet and ICT technology are actually used (see also Witte & Mannon, 2010). This meant that the social implications of technology were taken to a completely new level.

Notably, social media are not an entirely new phenomenon. Kaplan and Haenlein (2010) note that the term social media was already in use in the 1960s, though the current understanding of what constitutes social media is vastly different from those early days. Kaplan and Haenlein (2010) also argue that despite the close connection between Web 2.0 and social media, they are not in fact one and the same thing. Web 2.0 serves as an "ideological and technological foundation" (Kaplan & Haenlein, 2010, p. 61) for that which eventually became social media. They argue that from the point of view of average consumers, the most widely used applications can be listed as follows:

1　social networking sites (e.g. Facebook)
2　video-sharing sites (e.g. YouTube)
3　Wiki sites (information sites that can be freely accessed and edited by users, e.g. Wikipedia)
4　various forms of blogs (personal or microblogging sites such as Twitter)
5　virtual communities (e.g. Second Life)
6　online game communities (e.g. World of Warcraft).

What must be noted here is that despite their study being only a few years old, Kaplan and Haenlein's (2010) construction of social media is already slightly outdated. This serves as a clear example of the rapid pace at which social media continue to evolve as new services constantly emerge. Photo-sharing services such as Instagram are currently among the most popular social media applications, whereas the likes of Periscope, a live video-streaming service, is gaining popularity quickly as well. Present-day social media are thus becoming increasingly a live visual tool, serving as a window into the everyday lives of modern young and formerly young people alike. On the other hand, it could be argued that this is merely a natural progression from reality television, which has been around since the 1990s. Indeed, it is interesting to note that today many have the necessary tools to create content with a production value similar to content commercially mass produced. The result is the emergence of an entire industry based on social media content creation.

Another important aspect of the growing role of the different types of social media is that these services have also become important tools for constructing and shaping identity, particularly among young users. By posting pictures on Instagram, sharing a self-made video clip, commenting on Facebook, writing a blog or posting on Twitter, users are exploiting a multitude of methods for self-expression through customisable profiles. At the same time, these social tools are also a means for receiving feedback and constructing a form of dialogue over shared interests or relationship creation, for example. Returning to the highway metaphor, the two-way lane system provides tools for constructing and reshaping identity through self-expression, but it also allows modelling and self-adjustment through the reception of instant feedback from other users and desired groups (see also Buckingham, 2008; Kaplan & Haenlein, 2010). The role of social media has therefore become multilevel, being not merely a means for information retrieval and communication but also becoming central in the development of social identity and self-concept.

Past research indicates that young people are commonly the forerunners in adopting new trends and technologies (e.g. Pedersen, 2005) and this is the case with social media use as well. What makes today's young people particularly interesting is the fact that those born after the mid-1990s are the first generation after the commercialisation of the Internet. This means that many of today's young people have grown up being connected to a device or service, thus being highly integrated into the information society from a very young age (Boyd, 2014; Davies, Coleman & Livingstone, 2015; Lehdonvirta & Räsänen, 2011). Therefore, today's youth and young adults make a particularly interesting case from a research perspective for examining and gaining a better understanding of the role that the Internet, its social media and other forms of ICT play in their daily lives.

It is important to acknowledge that the influence of social media is not limited to individual users, as it is constantly taking a growing role in a much wider societal context. As an example, the US presidential election in 2008 was one of the first major political events that involved extensive online campaigning. For most elections today, particularly in Western societies, campaigning actively leverages various forms of social media. Social media have played a major role in political crises, such as the conflict between Russia and Ukraine (2014–), the Arab Spring (2011), the escalating situation in Syria (2011–) and the war on terrorism. During the London riots of 2011, various social media services were used extensively for the purposes of organising and guiding protesters to scenes of unrest. Social media outlets such as Twitter are used both as a live source of information by those desiring to be at the cutting edge of world events and as a dissemination tool for information management by those reporting from conflict zones where resources are particularly limited. Furthermore, terrorist organisations such as the Islamic State in Iraq and Syria (ISIS) are increasingly using social media for the purpose of spreading their propaganda.

These are just a few of the examples of what appears to be a constantly growing presence and influence of social media at different levels of the societal context. This development is the result of social media services being easy to use, conveniently accessible from all kinds of devices, and globally accessed by millions of users. Together, these tools enable users to meet needs and carry out connections with others in ways that have never before been possible at this scale of influence and efficiency.

1.3 Beyond social media

Social media in the societal context entail an ongoing, evolving process and as such it is difficult to predict what will happen next. New services, applications and platforms emerge constantly, yet no one can predict developments in the decades to come. What can be noted, however, is that the process is changing. That is, the core basis of different technologies and online platforms is already so extensive that most new updates are just that, updates of something already in use. Yet from a theoretical perspective, these new updates are significant, paving the way for another major shift from a Web 2.0 to a Web 3.0 society. If Web 1.0 served as a platform for the Internet to become a global medium, where users were largely just passengers in terms of information and content consumption, Web 2.0 brought forward the interactive role of the Internet, now known as social media. However, the transformation into a Web 3.0 society, in essence, involves an *accumulation of information* and how that information is processed within three different contexts: government, private sector and individual users.

In social media, we no longer make initial contact with other users purely on our own terms. Platform algorithms are increasingly making decisions for us, or at the very least we receive suggestions from the media concerning whom to contact and what new products we are likely to be interested in. Each and every Internet search is different, depending on the search engine one is using, where the search has been conducted and who carries it out. We, as users, may think that we are making independent decisions, but in reality a variety of algorithms are profiling us and trying to figure out who we are based on our behavioural patterns online. This is an issue that has become increasingly complicated for many desiring to seek out objective information that is not filtered on the basis of past consumption. Furthermore, this environmental mechanism can act to reinforce patterns of online behaviour unbeknownst to users.

To understand this accumulation of information better, we turn to two Internet heavyweights, Google and Facebook, taking a closer look at the very core of their revenue model system. Google, as most Internet users know, is by far the most commonly used online search engine developed by a company which has evolved to a multinational level and develops everything from search engines to self-driving cars. Facebook, on the other hand, is the most well-known and globally used social networking platform. Like Google, Facebook has also branched out from its original core product into a vast number of new, and in some cases innovative, social media services. Both of these companies are driven by a shared core idea dedicated to connecting users to both information and other people. From a certain point of view it is possible to argue that these two companies are merely providing free services that cater to some of the basic needs of their users. However, in order to grow and, most importantly, remain relevant and popular, both of these companies have had to build an efficient and productive revenue model. Thus, both Google and Facebook, like most Internet-based companies operating on the same playing field, base their revenue on the information they gain from users of their services. In practice, this means that these companies keep track of the online behaviour of those using their services, including their habits, interests, consumption and product preferences, whom they interact with online, and so on. This constant automatic information collection puts two and two together in a tireless manner, creating user behaviour profiles that are as accurate as possible.

What this process therefore embodies is an accumulation of information. In order to get an idea of the amount of information an individual user has "donated" over a period of a few years, the case of Maximilian Schrems provides a good frame of reference. An Austrian law student, Schrems claimed 1,222 pages of personal information from Facebook in 2011 in order to try to gain a better understanding of what the content regarding his social media activities was actually used for. Schrems has since taken legal action against Facebook on the basis of the company transferring information from the EU to the US and between its officials (O'Brian, 2012). Schrems is just one of the 1.59 billion active Facebook users (at the end of 2015). If each and every one of these users has even close to that amount of stored information about them, we can begin to get an idea of how far pattern-based information has accumulated on a global level.

Now, data collection and information use based on individual habits certainly constitute an interesting topic on their own, but this is not the core focus of our book. We will, however, return to it later in a discussion of negative consumption habits. Nonetheless, the aspect of cumulating online information in general provides a good gateway to understanding the increasing presence of hate in the online context. This entire process is illustrated in Figure 1.1.

The cumulation of information also means that existing content does not disappear. Rather, the information, both personal and general, once public, tends to remain at the disposal of other users. What this cumulating effect creates is what can be described as a type of *personalised online profile*. This profile tends to have two key elements, *permanence* and *externally controlled identity reinforcement*. What we mean by permanence is that the information provided by users, whether willingly (i.e. posting something on social media) or involuntarily through collection by service providers (as in the Google and Facebook revenue

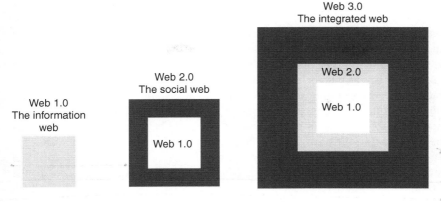

Figure 1.1 The accumulation of information on the Internet.

model described above), is difficult and in some cases even impossible to remove from the online sphere. By externally controlled identity reinforcement we mean search algorithms, the very same ones that dictate which results appear on Google searches, for example, based on past patterns of behaviour. Personalised profiles therefore consist of all the information that is available regarding any individual in the online context. This content does not disappear, but rather increases as information accumulates. Past actions, preferences and habits exist in a self-reinforcing cycle, as the algorithm promotes content that might be of interest based on previous habits. Furthermore, people with similar profiles receive similar promoted material, thus increasing links between like-minded users. "You might be interested in this" is an increasingly common suggestion that users come across when embarking on searches for news and other content. The search engine algorithms make sure that past user preferences dominate the type of information we continue to receive in the future.

What holds our interest here is the permanence of the content individuals themselves produce, particularly in association with hateful and harmful behaviour in the online context. In this context, references to hate speech are often introduced, igniting a relatively multileveled discourse. Notably, efforts have been made to define what constitutes hate speech in a more structured and empirical manner (Brown, 2015; Waldron, 2012). Yet, within public discourse, references to hate speech tend to be much more heated. Some argue for free speech, maintaining that individuals should be free to express their opinions about any topic of their choosing, whether it be religion, immigration, sexual orientation or otherwise. Others claim that there should be plenty of room for critical reflection regarding problems associated with, for instance, immigration or the threat of radical Islam. On the opposing side are those arguing that no such right exists when content inappropriately attacks certain groups of people, potentially inciting violence or prejudice against them.

We return to this discussion in greater detail in later chapters, but what we wish to bring forward briefly at this stage is the relationship between negative content and the online context. The reason for this is that the online context adds a different, and highly critical, dimension to hateful and harmful content in that it facilitates its development into something *toxic*. Our use of the term *toxic* is based not only on the nature of the content itself, but also on its longevity and continued danger. As such, toxic waste provides an effective parallel here. The fact that personal information and behavioural content cumulate online, combined with the difficulty of removing it, carries serious implications where the material is damaging. Material that is likely to have a negative impact on behaviour is no different, with widespread dissemination combined with difficulty of removal and little reduction of impact potential. Unlike past forms of large-scale accessible media, online hate material does not cycle out with the introduction of new material. The toxicity of its content can spread easily both early on and in perpetuity, carrying its original message with constant intensity and harming vulnerable targets.

1.4 Youth and culture of risk

The common reaction to many new and influential phenomena is generally two-fold. On the one hand, there is a level of excitement associated with the potential benefits and advancements, while on the other hand there is an equal sense of worry regarding what sorts of risk may be in store. Adoption of something new therefore tends to be a question of balancing between provided opportunities and associated risks (Livingstone & Helsper, 2010). The Internet and the technological mechanisms associated with it, along with the ever expanding number of different social media platforms, are a prime example of this. Here, the debate has been extensive and continues, revolving around the balancing of immense social and expressional benefits against the inherent risks of entering an arena with users set on causing harm to others.

The benefits of new technologies tend to include the increased opportunities for information access, learning and learning aids, social connections and new modes or capabilities associated with expression. The risks, on the other hand, include reliance on increasing screen time, lack of face-to-face interactions, privacy issues, cyberbullying, sexual soliciting, and all manner of targeted content aimed at causing harm. As noted earlier, younger users tend to be the earliest adopters as well as the most active users of new technologies. They also tend to be the highest-risk group when it comes to the potential dangers of these technologies. The reason for this is that young people are seen as less experienced when it comes to critically reflecting on the type of content facing them and the types of users because behaviours adopted during less mature developmental phases are reinforced, which potentially hinders access to beneficial content of a contrasting nature. Notably, existing research indicates that negative behaviour has become relatively commonplace in the online context, with sexual and other harassment, cyberbullying, soliciting and stalking becoming increasingly common (Näsi et al., 2014; Ortega et al., 2012; Sourander et al., 2010; Wolak, Finkelhor & Mitchell, 2012; Yar, 2013; Ybarra, Langhinrichsen-Rohling & Mitchell, 2016). Furthermore, various types of harmful content including pornography and extreme violence such as death sites have been found to constitute developmental risks for young users (see e.g. Gossett & Byrne, 2002; Tait, 2008; Ybarra & Mitchell, 2008). Finally, online communities focusing on pro-eating disorders, pro-self harm and pro-suicide are also increasingly common (e.g. Boyd, Ryan & Leavitt, 2011; Dunlop, More & Romer, 2011; Keipi, Oksanen, Hawdon, Näsi & Räsänen, 2015; Minkkinen et al., 2016; Oksanen et al., 2015).

Besides self-harm groups, there are various communities that glorify mass murderers, racist ideologies, xenophobia and radicalised political groups. Research has demonstrated their attractiveness to users seeking to commit radical acts such as school shootings (Oksanen, Hawdon & Räsänen, 2014). Statistically rare but socially and societally highly influential acts, such as the 2011 Norway attacks, have also been linked to online activism (Sandberg, Oksanen, Berntzen & Kiilakoski, 2014). The argument is at times put forth that these are relatively small groups and that only very few actually participate in the interaction and support represented causes. However, the nature of the Internet is such that even a small group of individuals can have a significant impact in the wider societal context due to the great potential for content exposure. As such, collective hate in the online context is not a particularly new phenomenon. The first major online hate site, Stormfront.com, was established in 1995 (Gerstenfeld, Grant & Chiang, 2003), with many prominent hate groups also going online during the 1990s. Furthermore, social media have played a significant role lately in bringing together like-minded people in the context of negative or risky behaviour.

Hate-motivated online communities and discussion forums are not only about fandom in support of a particular cause. The planned attack on the University of Helsinki in 2014, for instance, was discussed and planned in the anonymous Tor network throughout the previous year. The two culprits had become acquainted in the online platform earlier on, building on their shared interest in causing significant harm, making a violent transition from online hate to offline crime. Linked to this combining of dangerous like-minded users, earlier studies indicate that hate groups have been actively working to recruit young people through information technologies (e.g. Lee & Leets, 2002). Lately, there has been an even greater proliferation of online recruitment in connection with extremism. Various organised hate groups, from white supremacists to transnational jihadists, are active online (Brown, 2009). At present, one of the most notable of such groups is the aforementioned ISIS terrorist organisation. Groups such as ISIS have become a concern in Finland as well, as a significant number of jihadists have been recruited through social media from the different Nordic countries, with young males generally being the most likely recruits (see also Conway & McInerney, 2008). Therefore, the rise of social media has opened up additional avenues for promoting activism and radicalism and has also allowed a plethora of hate groups and terrorist organisations to flourish online (Oksanen, Hawdon & Räsänen, 2014).

1.5 The dividing Internet

It is important to state here that the Internet as such is not, and should not be, automatically perceived as something particularly deviant. What needs to be acknowledged, however, is how powerful a societal tool it is in serving both exposure to information and social interaction today. This further raises the notion that the Internet can cater to two very different aspects as a facilitator of user preferences. On the one hand, a number of positive aspects are absolutely central to online behaviour, such as convenient access to vast amounts of information, social connections, services and unique modes of expression. On the other hand, unsurprisingly, these same aspects can be used for very negative purposes. Paralleling Robert Louis Stevenson's literary classic, *The Strange Case of Dr. Jekyll and Mr. Hyde,* the Internet can bring out very different sides of its users. In assessing negative exposure, the question of balance emerges: do the positives outweigh the negatives and where do we draw the line? And, more importantly, can the negatives be controlled in an effective manner without undoing the benefits that depend on identical platforms and modes of expression?

One of the key aspects of this parallel with Dr Jekyll and Mr Hyde lies in the motives for users' behaviour. To what extent is content creation and type of interaction driven by users' needs to express themselves in certain ways? Is user behaviour being affected by the content or mechanisms of the online environment itself? As noted earlier, technology is now at the core of most Western societies, and, at least in theory, these technologies are first and foremost designed as tools to create a more efficient society. Yet the original premise of the Internet did not fully account for all the different human factors, especially in terms of negative effects. What we mean by this is that it has been difficult to predict how and to what extent people incorporate technology into their lives and, more importantly, how it will influence and dictate their behaviour. On the one hand, technology allows us to carry a small device that easily fits in a pocket and grants access to vast amounts of information and entertainment, yet at the same time the Internet can serve as a platform where the very worst in people can suddenly emerge.

The division between negative and positive has become a relatively distinctive feature of the present-day online environment, as it can be seen to serve a number of different personal and social contexts. Some seek out positive groups for support or validation while others seek to strengthen entrenched negative perceptions. The division can be seen as existing between access and no access, those who benefit and those who do not benefit, between those who agree and those who oppose. In the online context, a division between something positive and something negative can be expressed as a *digital divide.* This notion originates from the division between those who have access to the Internet and those who do not (e.g. Hargittai, 2002; see also Näsi, 2013), as those with access were perceived to be in a more privileged position than those without, due to the benefits of information and services available online.

However, over the years the definition of what constitutes a digital divide has evolved, mainly because access in general has become so much more common. The digital divide in many countries is therefore no longer about access but about user purposes (van Dijk, 2006). It is a division between those who use the Internet and ICTs for more practical purposes, such as information seeking and learning, and those who use it more for the purposes of entertainment, for example. A divide can also be made between social and anti-social behaviour, particularly in the context of polarised opinions and reactions to other users and content. The Internet therefore does possess the power to divide, not only bringing people together but also tearing them apart. In the sense that conflicts garner attention, it is not surprising that hate and harmful behaviour have become such a noted part of the online setting. Factors that explain the more traditional versions of the digital divide are relatively similar despite the evolving defini-tion. Past research has found that those better off in socio-economic terms tend to be those who have benefited more from the new technologies (e.g. Goldfarb & Prince, 2008; Koivusilta, Lintonen & Rimpelä, 2004). In the following empir-ical chapters we will examine whether similar factors help to explain the divi-sion between social and anti-social behaviour in the online context.

Another notable aspect of the present-day online communication and sociali-sation divide is a kind of compartmentalisation. In the online context, this com-partmentalisation has been referred to as a type of filter or social bubble (see e.g. Nikolov, Oliveira, Flammini & Menczer, 2015; Pariser, 2011). The notion of the bubble originates from one of the main premises of the Internet, which is to connect not only like-minded people but also users with information that is of interest. Thus, the bubble can be considered a space in which like-minded users are enclosed but also one that reaffirms users' pre-existing perspectives. Social media are particularly effective at creating and developing different bubbles by connecting both people and ideas on an immense scale.

According to Pariser (2011), a "filter bubble" is constructed on the basis of an individual's past online behaviour. The logic behind the filter bubble relies on the premise that users who are interested in a specific topic are then targeted with content that fits their profile, and as a result content contrary to their views or interests is filtered away (Pariser, 2011). This also relates to our earlier discus-sion about the revenue models of social media operators and online search engines, along with the constant collection of information based on users' online behaviour in order to construct personalised user profiles. However, research appears not to support the idea of a filter bubble as a particularly dominant force in cutting people off from information that does not reinforce their existing views (e.g. Nguyen, Hui, Harper, Teryeen & Konstan, 2014; Zuiderveen Borge-sius et al., 2016). Therefore, the bubble appears to serve more as a communal feature, bringing like-minded people together. However, according to Abisheva, Garcia and Schweitzer (2016), it is the bursting or collision of different types of filter bubbles that fosters increasing polarisation and negativity in the online context. That is, one's views and ideology grow stronger within the bubble, yet in doing so reinforce separation from those who do not share similar perceptions or ideology. Therefore, from the perspective of social cohesion, the premise in many online social interactions is already such that it is much easier to get into an argument about who is right and who is wrong than it is to find some form of common ground.

The dark side of the Internet is increasingly evident. It has a whole host of different characteristics and can involve individual actors as well as larger groups dedicated to a particular cause. In this book our focus is on the darker aspects of the Internet and social media in particular. Our goal is therefore to provide new information, from both theoretical and empirical perspectives, on the hate aspects of the Internet. In the following chapters we focus in more detail on different aspects of online hate. We first build a theoretical map of online hate by linking key theories from criminology, sociology and social psychology with forms of hate in the new online context. We then take a closer look at rising hate online, including hate groups, individual actors and created content prominent in routine contexts. We also present an empirical overview of hate in a cross-national context, as we look into exposure to hate material and its implications in four Western countries, namely the UK, the US, Germany and Finland. Building on these components of past theory and empirical findings concerning hate, we also present a novel model of online hate dynamics in terms of identity and behavioural patterns linked to environmental factors prevalent online, all towards bridging past theory with current online realities. Finally, we delve into the social spheres of hate online to establish a deeper understanding of the bigger picture of hate today and where we may be headed in terms of social media and the management of risk.

References

Abisheva, A., Garcia, D., & Schweitzer, F. (2016). When the filter bubble bursts: Collective evaluation dynamics in online communities. Submitted to the Eighth International ACM Web Science Conference 2016. Retrieved from http://arxiv.org/pdf/1602.05642v1.pdf.

Bell, D. (1973). The coming of the post-industrial society. *The Educational Forum, 40*(4), 574–579. DOI: 10.1080/00131727609336501.

Bittman, M., Rice, J. M., & Wajcman, J. (2004). Appliances and their impact: The ownership of domestic technology and time spent on household work. *The British Journal of Sociology, 55*(3), 401–423. DOI: 10.1111/j.1468-4446.2004.00026.x.

Boyd, D. (2014). *It's Complicated: The Social Lives of Networked Teens*. New Haven, CT: Yale University Press.

Boyd, D., Ryan, J., & Leavitt, A. (2011). Pro-self-harm and the visibility of youth-generated problematic content. *I/S: A Journal of Law and Policy for the Information Society, 7*(1), 1–31. Retrieved from www.danah.org/papers/2011/IS-ProSelfHarm.pdf.

Brown, A. (2015). *Hate Speech Law: A Philosophical Examination* (Vol. 67). New York: Routledge.

Brown, C. (2009). WWW.HATE.COM: White supremacist discourse on the Internet and the construction of whiteness ideology. *Howard Journal of Communications, 20*(2), 189–208. DOI: 10.1080/10646170902869544.

Buckingham, D. (Ed.) (2008). *Youth, Identity, and Digital Media*. The John D. and Catherine T. MacArthur Foundation Series on Digital Media and Learning. Cambridge, MA: MIT Press. DOI: 10.1162/dmal.9780262524834.vii.

Castells, M., & Himanen, P. (2002). *The Information Society and the Welfare State: The Finnish Model*. New York: Oxford University Press. DOI: 10.1093/acprof:oso/978019 9256990.001.0001.

Conway, M., & McInerney, L. (2008). Jihadi video and auto-radicalisation: Evidence from an exploratory YouTube study. In D. Ortiz-Arroyo, H. L. Larsen, D. D. Zeng, D. Hicks & G. Wagner (Eds.), *Intelligence and Security Informatics: First European Conference, EuroISI 2008, Esbjerg, Denmark, December 3–5, 2008, Proceedings* (pp. 108–118). Berlin: Springer-Verlag Berlin Heidelberg. DOI: 10.1007/978-3-540-89900-6_13.

Cowan, R. S. (1976). The "industrial revolution" in the home: Household technology and social change in the 20th century. *Technology and Culture, 17*(1), 1–23. DOI: 10.2307/3103251.

Davies, C., Coleman, J., & Livingstone, S. (Eds.) (2015). *Digital Technologies in the Lives of Young People*. New York: Routledge.

Dunlop, S. M., More, E., & Romer, D. (2011). Where do youth learn about suicides on the Internet, and what influence does this have on suicidal ideation? *Journal of Child Psychology and Psychiatry, 52*(10), 1073–1080. DOI: 10.1111/j.1469-7610.2011.02416.x.

Gerstenfeld, P. B., Grant, D. R., & Chiang, C.-P. (2003). Hate online: A content analysis of extremist Internet sites. *Analyses of Social Issues and Public Policy, 3*(1), 29–44. DOI: 10.1111/j.1530-2415.2003.00013.x.

Goldfarb, A., & Prince, J. (2008). Internet adoption and usage patterns are different: Implications for the digital divide. *Information Economics and Policy, 20*(1), 2–15. DOI: 10.1016/j.infoecopol.2007.05.001.

Gossett, J. L., & Byrne, S. (2002). "Click here": A content analysis of Internet rape sites. *Gender & Society, 16*(5), 689–709. DOI: 10.1177/089124302236992.

Hargittai, E. (2002). Second-level digital divide: Differences in people's online skills. *First Monday, 7*(4–1). DOI: 10.5210/fm.v7i4.942.

Kaplan, A. M., & Haenlein, M. (2010). Users of the world, unite! The challenges and opportunities of social media. *Business Horizons, 53*(1), 59–68. DOI: 10.1016/j. bushor.2009.09.003.

Keipi, T., Oksanen, A., Hawdon, J., Näsi, M., & Räsänen, P. (2015). Harm-advocating online content and subjective well-being: A cross-national study of new risks faced by youth. *Journal of Risk Research, 18*, 1–16. DOI: 10.1080/13669877.2015.1100660.

Koivusilta, L, Lintonen, T., & Rimpelä, A. (2004) Digitaalinen eriarvoisuus – IKT:n käyttöorientaatiot sosiodemografisen taustan, koulutusurien ja terveyden suhteen [in Finnish]. In M. Lehtonen & H. Ruokamo (Eds.), *Lapin tietoyhteiskuntaseminaari, tutkijatapaamisen artikkelikirja 2004* (pp. 97–106).

Lawson-Borders, G. (2003). Integrating new media and old media. *International Journal on Media Management, 5*(2), 91–99. DOI: 10.1080/14241270309390023.

Lee, E., & Leets, L. (2002). Persuasive storytelling by hate groups online: Examining its effects on adolescents. *American Behavioral Scientist, 45*(6), 927–957. DOI: 10.1177/0002764202045006003.

Lehdonvirta, V., & Räsänen, P. (2011). How do young people identify with online and offline peer groups? A comparison between UK, Spain, and Japan. *Journal of Youth Studies, 14*(1), 91–108. DOI: 10.1080/13676261.2010.506530.

Lievrouw, L. (2004) What's changed about new media? Introduction to the fifth anniversary issue of *New Media & Society*. *New Media & Society, 6*(1), 9–15. DOI: 10.1177/1461444804039898.

Livingstone, S. (1999). New media, new audiences? *New Media & Society, 1*(1), 59–66. DOI: 10.1177/1461444899001001010.

Livingstone, S., & Helsper, E. (2010). Balancing opportunities and risks in teenagers' use of the Internet: The role of online skills and Internet self-efficacy. *New Media & Society, 12*(2), 309–329. DOI: 10.1177/1461444809342697.

Minkkinen, J., Oksanen, A., Näsi, M., Keipi, T., Kaakinen, M., & Räsänen, P. (2016). Does social belonging to primary groups protect young people from the effects of pro-suicide sites?. *Crisis, 37*(1), 31–41. DOI: 10.1027/0227-5910/a000356.

Nguyen, T. T., Hui, P. M., Harper, F. M., Teryeen, L., & Konstan, J. A. (2014). Exploring the filter bubble: The effect of using recommender systems on content diversity. In *Proceedings of the 23rd International Conference on World Wide Web* (pp. 677–686). New York: ACM. DOI: 10.1145/2566486.2568012.

Nikolov, D., Oliveira, D. F., Flammini, A., & Menczer, F. (2015). Measuring online social bubbles. *PeerJ Computer Science 1*, e38. DOI: 10.7717/peerj-cs.38.

Näsi, M. (2013). *ICT Disparities in Finland – Access and Implications*. Turku: University of Turku, Annales Universitatis.

Näsi, M., Räsänen, P., Oksanen, A., Hawdon, J., Keipi, T., & Holkeri, E. (2014). Association between online harassment and exposure to harmful online content: A cross-national comparison between the United States and Finland. *Computers in Human Behavior, 41*(December), 137–145. DOI: 10.1016/j.chb.2014.09.019.

O'Brian, K. J. (2012, 5 February). Austrian law student faces down Facebook. *New York Times*. Retrieved from www.nytimes.com/2012/02/06/technology/06iht-rawdata06.html?_r=0.

O'Reilly, T. (2005, 30 September) What is Web 2.0? Design patterns and business models for the next generation of software. Retrieved from http://oreilly.com/web2/archive/what-is-web-20.html.

Oksanen, A., Garcia, D., Sirola, A., Näsi, M., Kaakinen, M., Keipi, T., & Räsänen, P. (2015). Pro-anorexia and anti-pro-anorexia videos on YouTube: Sentiment analysis of user responses. *Journal of Medical Internet Research, 17*(11), e256. DOI: 10.2196/jmir.5007.

Oksanen, A., Hawdon, J., & Räsänen, P. (2014). Glamorizing rampage online: School shooting fan communities on YouTube. *Technology in Society, 39*, 55–67. DOI: 10.1016/j.techsoc.2014.08.001.

Ortega, R., Elipe, P., Mora-Merchan, J., Brighi, A., Guarini, A., Smith, P., Thompson, F., & Tippett, N. (2012). The emotional impact of bullying and cyberbullying on victims: A European cross-national study. *Aggressive Behaviour, 38*(5), 342–356. DOI: 10.1002/ab.21440.

Pariser, E. (2011). *The Filter Bubble: What the Internet Is Hiding from You*. New York: Penguin Press.

Pedersen, P. E. (2005). Adoption of mobile Internet services: An exploratory study of mobile commerce early adopters. *Journal of Organizational Computing and Electronic Commerce, 15*(3), 203–222. DOI: 10.1207/s15327744joce1503_2.

Pratt, T. C., Holtfreter, K., & Reisig, M. D. (2010). Routine online activity and Internet fraud targeting: Extending the generality of routine activity theory. *Journal of Research in Crime and Delinquency*, 47(3), 267–296. DOI: 10.1177/0022427810365903.

Reyns, B. W. (2013). Online routines and identity theft victimisation: Further expanding routine activity theory beyond direct-contact offenses. *Journal of Research in Crime and Delinquency, 50*(2), 216–238. DOI: 10.1177/0022427811425539.

Sandberg, S., Oksanen, A., Berntzen, L. E., & Kiilakoski, T. (2014). Stories in action: The cultural influences of school shootings on the terrorist attacks in Norway. *Critical Studies on Terrorism, 7*(2), 277–296. DOI: 10.1080/17539153.2014.906984.

Sourander, A., Klomek, A. B., Ikonen, M., Lindroos, J., Luntamo, T., Koskelainen, M. et al. (2010). Psychosocial risk factors associated with cyberbullying among adolescents: A population-based study. *Archives of General Psychiatry, 67*(7), 720–728. DOI: 10.1001/archgenpsychiatry.2010.79.

Spears, R., Postmes, T., Lea, M., & Wolbert, A. (2002). When are net effects gross products? The power of influence and the influence of power in computer-mediated communication. *Journal of Social Issues, 58*(1), 91–107. DOI: 10.1111/1540-4560.00250.

Tait, S. (2008). Pornographies of violence? Internet spectatorship on body horror. *Critical Studies in Media Communication, 25*(1), 91–111. DOI: 10.1080/15295030701851148.

van Dijk, J. A. G. M. (2006). Digital divide research, achievements and shortcomings. *Poetics, 34*(4–5), 221–235. DOI: 10.1016/j.poetic.2006.05.004.

van Dijk, J. A. G. M. (2012). *The Network Society* (3rd edn). London: Sage.

Waldron, J. (2012). *The Harm in Hate Speech.* Cambridge, MA: Harvard University Press.

Witte, J. C., & Mannon, S. E. (2010). *The Internet and Social Inequalities.* New York: Routledge.

Wolak, J., Finkelhor, D., & Mitchell, K. J. (2012). How often are teens arrested for sexting? Data from a national sample of police cases. *Pediatrics, 129*(1), 4–12. DOI: 10.1542/peds.2011-2242.

Yar, M. (2013). *Cybercrime and Society.* London: Sage Publications.

Ybarra, M. L., Langhinrichsen-Rohling, J., & Mitchell, K. J. (2016). Stalking-like behaviour in adolescence: Prevalence, intent, and associated characteristics. *Psychology of Violence.* Advance online publication. DOI: 10.1037/a0040145.

Ybarra, M. L., & Mitchell, K. J. (2008). How risky are social networking sites? A comparison of places online where youth sexual solicitation and harassment occurs. *Pediatrics, 121*(2), e350-e357. DOI: 10.1542/peds.2007-0693.

Zuiderveen Borgesius, F. J., Trilling, D., Moeller, J., Bodó, B., De Vreese, C. H., & Helberger, N. (2016). Should we worry about filter bubbles?. *Internet Policy Review, 5*(1). DOI: 10.14763/2016.1.401.

2 Social media and identity

2.1 Expanded interaction and social media

The ways in which online hate functions today is a product of both user intent and the mechanisms available for making that content available. Online, users can express themselves to a potentially global audience in ways that were not possible just a decade ago. The matching of user intent with the tools available for disseminating content can result in wide-reaching effects even without specific audience targeting. An understanding of hateful intent and methods of how that intent can be delivered requires a contextual look at the users themselves through tried and true theoretical frameworks used in past research of the offline setting especially. Deep motivations and needs that drive users to seek out validation through communities or content dissemination can shed valuable insight into how and why certain behaviour is carried out online. As such, past theory on identity is helpful for grasping the motivations, needs and social context of the individual user, along with the environmental factors and tools available to the user to influence others.

The interactions and social dynamics of self-perception carried out offline have of course been the focus of a great majority of past theory. The extent to which those theories are useful in the online social space is of interest here. In terms of peer recognition offline, for example, self-presentation to a desired peer group may be key to gaining acceptance. This can involve attitudes, appearance or mirrored behavioural norms. The audience receiving this self-presentation offline is tied to the element of physical presence, which then determines the scope of influence. If a new member of a peer group seeks to gain favour, the feedback loops are straightforward in the sense that physical space is shared and expression is transferred directly between parties. Indeed, word of mouth can also spread information beyond the initial social setting. Furthermore, risk may result from seeking attention from those uninterested in accepting the individual concerned. Social Identity Theory (SIT) does well to map the dynamics at play here, but what might this same process look like online?

In the online setting, the key dynamics of this scenario remain highly relevant; a desired group is targeted for validation seeking, group norms are assessed and self-presentation is tailored in a fashion pleasing to the desired

[handwritten: more self tailoring online]

identity group. However, the degree to which the self can be tailored online extends far beyond that available offline. The lack of physical presence can be leveraged to highlight aspects of the self that may not be accurate. Furthermore, the accuracy of displayed identity characteristics may not be verifiable by the group itself due to the inability to interact physically with the user. Online, reputation effects can also be managed in a way less possible offline as versions of oneself need not overlap. Online identities can be created and deleted easily. One can begin anew and even reinforce new attempts without disclosing unfavourable experiences and impressions left with other groups online. Furthermore, the sphere of influence in terms of who is able to find a customised online self can be global. Profiles created for specific purposes of validation, as in this example, can also be targeted based on the very characteristics that were meant to attract positive attention. Indeed, the dynamics of validation seeking from identity groups online and offline are quite similar. However, certain enabling tools of the online setting can also be used to enhance areas previously less malleable.

[handwritten: theory/tools outdated to match social dynamics online]

Although the individual needs of users remain similar to those of the days before wide-scale social media use, the theoretical frameworks used in past research are not quite up to the task of framing the realities of the online setting adequately due to key areas of social dynamics that are closely tied to the enabling tools of the Internet. This is especially true in terms of the scope of access to others and the extent to which some level of lessened identifiability or visibility can be a factor in expression and interaction. Today, users have access to the world through social media platforms where they can present themselves as they please, yet are also subject to the targeting and reactions of a potentially massive audience. It seems reasonable to ask: are the online and offline social environments equivalent in the degree to which they offer a neutral setting for exploration and expression?

[handwritten: ✳ This chap will...]

We will identify social aspects of the Internet environment that are central to identity and link them to various themes of social identity theory (Tajfel & Turner, 1979) and related approaches to better understand the dynamics relevant to the online setting. This theory is an excellent starting point as it helps to frame an understanding of the individual despite perhaps lacking the scope to tackle the dynamic social setting available online today. Yet it acts as a stepping stone to the development of a novel theoretical approach applicable to the online environment prominent today.

As the previous chapter illustrated, the Internet has become a central aspect of daily life for much of the Western world in terms of connecting a significant portion of both the social and the personal. Interaction is increasingly mediated by the online medium, where enhanced forms of expression, relationship management and socialisation are possible. Here, the scale of social networks can be increased and decreased depending on the desired audience size. Social media allow for new forms of customising relationships and interaction with other users, as user profiles, interest groups and modes of communication can vary according to the preferences of the users themselves. Furthermore, the online environment continues to branch out as its users manage and develop expressional content and communities through efficient and convenient communication. This represents a truly dynamic setting where content creation, relationship management and social network scale can all be managed by users through interaction whose forms can also vary.

A central aspect of this adoption of technological outlets is the social aspect of becoming connected to others. The popular modes of expression and interaction online reflect the relational desires and needs that exist offline. The Internet is the meeting place of the world, and has been for some time. It continues to evolve, as do the users with whom it is most popular. The relational aspects of the Internet are consumed by young generations at a rate far surpassing other demographics (Lehdonvirta & Räsänen, 2011; Näsi, Räsänen & Lehdonvirta, 2011). Today, users have the option to start their day by expressing sentiments to thousands or even millions if their social network scale so allows. Opinions, attitudes and norms on any number of issues can be affirmed or denied, targeting any number of specific or general audiences at a moment's notice. Key social identities can thereby be reinforced at a pace and scale previously reserved for the social or cultural elite. Furthermore, whether those with whom one interacts are considered close friends or unknown followers depends on the user in question. As such, the variance in expressional and relational forums online is vast.

Indeed, though the capability exists, the majority of users do not have direct expressional access to millions or even thousands. Social networks online are important reinforcements of what happens offline as well, creating convenience in communication and reinforcing relationships already existing offline. Here, convenient access to others is sought, rather than access to a wider audience. However, the convenience and scale can work together for those targeting certain groups for damaging purposes. Thus, central to this popularity with young people is the aspect of being able to seek out relational benefit from others, which affords new opportunities for identity development, social exploration and new methods for expression (Keipi & Oksanen, 2014). Online, users can explore who they are by learning, interacting and independently seeking out the fulfilment of various needs that they hold, especially socially. The Internet provides countless platforms from which to express oneself, seek feedback and develop opinions concerning anything imaginable. However, as mentioned earlier, these new opportunities available online can bring new forms of risk to users. Just as offline interaction brings various negative experiences, the same is true online. Harassment, targeted hate and bullying of various levels of severity are prevalent throughout the Internet, as users take advantage of the ease of communication and effective platforms that are otherwise used in beneficial ways (Festl & Quandt, 2013; Wegge, Vandebosch, Eggermont & Walrave, 2015).

In this online setting, users are empowered to choose social frameworks in a way that has not been possible before. Individuals are often limited by what they know. More specifically, aspects of the self may not be explored if the potential of similar others is unknown. Here, validation seeking may not be prioritised in important developmental ways where sought-after identity groups are inaccessible. Online, access to others is made easy, as is seeking out like-minded

Customized Self Presentation

communities. On the Internet, social support and a desired form of validation may be only one click away, as so much is within anyone's reach. As a social tool, the Internet is unparalleled in its flexibility in meeting users' needs. Central to this usefulness in finding validation is the possibility of customisable self-presentation (Hogan, 2010); these methods of connectedness and expression chosen by users act as signposts towards identifying various needs whose fulfilment is being sought. Online, users and communities of users can clearly identify themselves as they wish through social media. Here, like-minded networks can be conveniently found and joined. One result of the expressional benefits and access to others online is the presence of countless accessible social spheres revolving around all imaginable shared characteristics; in the online setting, the variety of available identity-reinforcing groups is unparalleled.

if offline no belong go online

This freedom of movement online can empower users by providing more convenient ways to strengthen a sense of independence through encouraging fulfilling forms of expression. Online interaction can bring new opportunities for relating to like-minded individuals or communities. These benefits can be most valued by those who seek a sense of belonging that perhaps may not be as accessible offline (Blais, Craig, Pepler & Connolly, 2008). These online mechanisms can be unique to the setting or can be an extension of the setting already present offline. The environment provided by the Internet can be used, on a more personal level, for entertainment, escapism, learning or any number of other experiences depending on the user in question.

Social media, as mapped out in the previous chapter, provide the backdrop for the dynamics with which we are concerned here. This multifaceted environment for interaction and expression hosts all manner of positive, neutral and damaging material. As a whole, social media make up the most used portion of the Internet (Wang & Stefanone, 2013). Linked to its popularity is the availability of like-minded interactive partners and personally discoverable interest-based groups (Keipi & Oksanen, 2014). Here, access and personal identification add to the relational possibilities being sought by many users and set the stage for the realities of online hate. Social media platforms such as Facebook can thus be used in any number of ways: from maintaining offline relationships with those who already know the user in question, to creating a global network of new connections based on a customised and exaggerated profile in the search for validation or self-gratification.

managing old + create new identities

Just as in the offline world, communities of like-minded individuals form organically, as users balance a desire for connection and strengthening of shared interests. Online groups can provide reinforcement to users' identity expression and exploration, complementing the mechanisms affecting the individual offline as well (Davidson & Martelozzo, 2013). Identity development is a key motivator in seeking out a sense of worth and importance from desired groups online, especially when interests are shared (Panek, Nardis & Konrath, 2013). Significantly, these online communities can also reinforce negative effects, for example through the production and targeting of damaging material and sentiment (Oksanen, Hawdon, Holkeri, Näsi & Räsänen, 2014). The mechanisms of the online setting that can also be used for beneficial connectedness and group reinforcement can also be leveraged to encourage negative effects for targeted groups (Näsi et al., 2014). The effects of these groups can be extensive, including motivating extreme forms of violence and hatred among users (Oksanen, Hawdon & Räsänen, 2014). The scale of both the positive and the negative potential of online groups and user activity is dependent on the fulfilment of the needs of participants. An understanding of those needs allows for a clarified view of why social behaviour online takes the forms considered most prevalent, especially in terms of expression, seeking validation and group formation.

2.2 Social identity theory and the online setting

When delving into hate material and the targeting of groups, we simultaneously encounter the issue of group dynamics. Namely, we are dealing with sides that oppose one another, and this requires a contextual understanding of where group associations come from and what purposes they serve. The foundation of an understanding of group formation and socialisation in general, in terms of both the online and the offline settings, requires a perspective rooted in the concept of identity and how a sense of self develops. This opens the discussion to delving into why group formation matters and what characteristics unique to the online setting might affect the dynamics of that fundamental socialisation and resulting expression in the form of both positive and, especially, negative content. In a discussion of the animosity between individuals or groups with targeted identities, an understanding of the dynamics actively driving such interaction becomes necessary.

SIT helps us to map out the dynamics driving popular forms of social media activity while also highlighting areas of the online environment that are beyond its scope and thus require a new complementary contribution. SIT was originally developed by British social psychologists Henri Tajfel and John Turner (1979, 1986). This highly regarded theory was based on both Tajfel's and Turner's empirical work in the early 1970s (e.g. Tajfel, 1972, 1974; Turner, 1975), where they brought forth a great deal of innovation on social categorisation and intergroup relations. The term SIT was coined in 1978 by Turner and Brown, and further developed by Turner who continued working on the theory after the death of Tajfel in 1982 (Turner & Brown, 1978; Turner & Reynolds, 2010).

According to Tajfel and Turner (1979), people categorise themselves and others to make their world understandable and they identify with these categories and use them to make social comparisons between different groups. In other words, SIT is concerned with group phenomena within the individual and makes the assumption that a notable source of self-concept is determined by one's belonging to various social groups while also discriminating against other unfavoured groups. These memberships are then categorised internally by individuals, who also categorise the affiliations of others, all the while evaluating the interplay between them. Furthermore, the development of a positive social identity is central to the motivation to foster favourable group memberships by displaying behaviour rewarded by desired groups. Thus, groups have behavioural norms which also distinguish them from others. SIT was grounded on a minimal group paradigm, through finding that the simple act of categorising the self and others into groups causes discrimination against outsiders and favouritism towards one's own in terms of how resources and sentiment are distributed (Billig, 2002; Turner & Reynolds, 2010). Despite the minimal conditions of early experiments, where participant groups were randomly assigned to interact without face-to-face contact, the study led to this clear delineation between favouring and discriminating.

As such, one's identity is continually evolving through countless comparisons and negotiations between the self and what or whom one experiences (Abrams & Hogg, 2004; Jenkins, 2004). Here, the individual and his or her social context are continually interacting, giving and taking, while forming the next version of the self. Aspects of the self evolve as the self-concept develops through social contact. As individuals carry out this process while approving or disapproving of all manner of content and behaviour, a sense of self in relation to others takes shape in new ways and can lead the individual to norms that reinforce past values and group affiliations (Thoits, Virshup, Lauren & Ashmore, 1997). As such, identity is social by nature and formed through interacting with various environments. It is the contrast between the individual and the social environment that shapes one's core identifications. Thus, we make decisions of who we are based on our preferences, what we know and the other possibilities that are available to us.

SIT (Tajfel & Turner, 1979) frames this development of the individual within a social context and through that helps to explain why interaction is important to users, along with the dynamics of group formation and validation so central to popular forms of online behaviour. Put simply, social identity is the foundation that connects an individual to the social group. It represents a sharing of core values or motivations that strengthens social bonds to the point of adopting a group's identity. Here, similarities and differences are identified between the self and others. This comparison begins a continual interplay between how others identify with an individual and how that individual identifies with those others (Turner, 1975). This process is one of continual comparison, being set into motion by recognising familiar aspects in others. Here, individuals form an idea of their social environment through categorising themselves and others into groups, while also establishing a favourable view of their own group and finding self-concept and emotional significance with membership. This represents the social self, and can take many forms, limited only by the number of group associations that are available today.

As such, SIT is a major part of a rich empirical research corpus showing the human need for social belonging (see Baumeister & Leary, 1995). As users navigate the social landscape online, comparison is a continual process through which users determine favourable and unfavourable identity characteristics. This exploration is centrally motivated by a drive to experience a sense of validation and significance (Tajfel, 1979). Thus, as in the offline setting, social identity online is the individual's knowledge of belonging to a social group combined with a sense of significance attributed to that membership. Here, points of reference in terms of where one fits into society at large are created through identifying with others.

Perceptions of others and how one is perceived by others influence the comparison process (Tajfel, 1981). This sense of self-concept developed through one's social identity is founded in a sense of membership. And, as a multiplicity of memberships is a regular part of socialisation, it is the interaction of multiple identity group memberships that shapes one's self-concept (Jenkins, 2004). This involves a great deal of role adoption depending on the norms of a group, where the individual adapts to new social contexts and group expectations. Notably, these groups can exist at all sorts of different social levels, from society-wide to professional and from cultural to interest-based (Hogg, Terry & White, 1995). In addition, the social space provided by the Internet in the form of social media allows for an interesting combination of comparative factors that has, in the past, been far less accessible. Online, not only can identity characteristics be compared in the development of one's own social identity, but the size and composition of the social networks of others also become a point of comparison. Individuals' social networks and scope of influence are highly visible in the form of friend lists on Facebook, followers on Instagram, or subscribers on YouTube, for example. These points of comparison can be leveraged for validation in any number of ways, as the size of social influence can be effectively displayed in a concrete and easily understandable way.

Throughout all of these various social group memberships and comparisons that can lead to discovering favourable identities, communication remains absolutely central. Online, the number of available contacts, interest-based communities, and identity group variations is second to none. Furthermore, the tools of communication accessible there are beyond anything available offline in terms of efficiency and convenience. These two aspects of the online setting, namely interactive partners and access to those users and their content, can motivate higher levels of interaction with both known and unknown partners, thus broadening the scope of social contrast and points of comparison in the development of self-concept. Where communication is made more convenient and the need for social interaction for various needs is present, development is enabled that might otherwise have been slowed or even put aside in favour of something less challenging.

Central to the discussion thus far has been the issue of how an individual's perceptions can shift in the process towards identifying with certain groups. As identity groups become more defined and simultaneously more distinct from one another, how one views oneself can also shift and develop to a point otherwise unlikely. As such, a further development of social identity theory relevant to our discussion here concerning online phenomena is that of self-categorisation, or how an individual's perception of self evolves according to determined ingroups and outgroups. This takes the previously mentioned aspect of identity development through comparison and categorisation a step further. As an individual comes to form a sense of ingroup and outgroup, a process of categorisation occurs where members of groups are simplified into representatives of the assigned groups. Here, self-categorisation creates social identity processes through the stereotyping of the self and others (Turner, 1985). As one adopts the norms of a group, distinctions develop between "us" and "others". But how do members determine a point of comparison or standard by which the group is measured and therefore also compared to others? This point of comparison is known as the identity prototype, a representation of attributes embodied by the group in question.

This plays out in practice in many ways throughout all levels of society. Political parties have their prototypical representative, sports teams have their mascots or star players, countries have national heroes and religions have an embodiment of a way of life. As one navigates the multitude of identity groups throughout various social settings, categorisation is a continuous process, one heavily influenced by oversimplification. Here, identity characteristics are stereotyped according to a perceived prototype. This involves simplifying complex individuals who are members of a certain group into a stereotypical caricature informed by a group prototype. Furthermore, the identity prototype of a group displays features typical of group membership. In practice, this can be a representation of members who most accurately reflect the group or idealised combinations of group norms or features. Central to the prototype's value to the group is in the provision of an example of attributes that distinguish the group in question from others, whether through beliefs, behaviours or attitudes; here, the prototype polarises similarities and differences between groups in order to ensure the group's unique standing. Notably, this role can be actual or imagined by those associated with a certain identity group.

In the realm of hate content, a prototype can be used to validate and even inspire damaging action, as behaviour and attitudes can be looked up to as something to be admired by other members while also motivating the production of hate content. The prototype reduces uncertainty in these cases by determining boundaries and practical definitions for group cohesion (Hogg & Terry, 2001). Notably, prototypes tend to be more attractive as idealised examples during times of uncertainty; fear can drive individuals to the simplifying effects of stereotypical or norm-inducing prototypes. For example, during times of crisis, minorities have been used as a scapegoat by national prototypes to direct oversimplified views of cause and effect, resulting in widespread human rights violations. This pattern of upholding a prototype, reinforcement of group norms, and shared action among the group towards the "other" can be seen in all manner of social identity interaction from race wars to sporting events.

2.3 From individual self to group self

In terms of social identity, there is a shift from thinking in terms of being an individual to thinking in terms of one's group identity. This process is one of depersonalisation, as one becomes to some extent absorbed into a group self, for example through adopting new behavioural norms. It is important to note that depersonalisation is linked to an earlier theoretical phenomenon known as deindividuation, which means immersion of the individual in a group identity to the point of losing individual identity through a social form of anonymity (Lea & Spears, 1991). This early view of a loss of self rather than a simple shift in self-awareness to the group level provides a foundation for a balanced view of the effects of group identity.

Even before the development of the Internet and the various levels of customised visibility there, anonymity was considered a central component of some of the most powerful forms of collective behaviour (Reicher, 1987). Here, anonymity refers to instances where individuals are so deeply identified as part of a group that they are absorbed to the point of becoming free from individual behavioural accountability. Notably, deindividuation theory was an attempt to explain the violence of crowds and the irrationality of mobs. Deindividuation assumes that because anonymity removes interpersonal cues, it also decreases attention to others, creating a level of impersonality that acts to promote conflict and negative behaviours (Singer, Brush & Lublin, 1965; Zimbardo, 1969). Here, reduced self-awareness is considered central to facilitating negative behaviours due to the freedom from accountability that can result from hiding identifiability, distilled as "disinhibited behaviour" (Walther, 1996). This loss of self results in a weakening of one's sense of individuality when socially unacceptable behaviour becomes attractive due to relative freedom from social norms. In practice, this can take many forms; identifying with a group and acting as a representative can result in behaviours beyond what one might consider acceptable otherwise.

Zimbardo, one of the early pioneers of deindividuation theory, carried out experimental research that helps to illustrate the issue. In one experiment (Zimbardo, 1969), one set of participants were made anonymous by wearing clothing similar to the uniform of the Ku Klux Klan (KKK) while others were identifiable through normal clothing with nametags. Both groups of participants were directed individually to cause pain to a target; results indicated that those under the veil of anonymity were more likely to cause harm driven by externally imposed instructions. Here, a loss of individuality and personal responsibility seemed to drive harmful action that might otherwise not have been carried out. As such, central in deindividuation research was seeking an explanation for the negative behaviour of violent or otherwise damaging groups of people (Diener, 1979).

However, not all outcomes of research on anonymity tied to deindividuation were destructive in nature, as decreased aggression and increased affection through anonymity were also found (Gergen, Gergen & Barton, 1973; Johnson & Downing, 1979). Furthermore, increased self-awareness, enhanced decision-making and even decreases in disinhibition were also observed in other studies (Lea & Spears, 1991; Matheson & Zanna, 1988). As such, deindividuation can occur in any number of settings for either positive or negative ends: from military units, gangs and cults to sports teams, law enforcement and political parties. Central here is the role of group cohesion in promoting certain norms which can indeed be either positive or negative.

The social identity component of depersonalisation builds upon the loss of self discovered through early research into deindividuation phenomena. Here, depersonalisation refers to a shift in thinking from individual self to the group member self, rather than a loss of self as put forth by deindividuation. Deindividuation predicts negative behaviour, yet anonymity was found to result in positive outcomes as well. Depersonalisation helps to explain this contradiction in effects. As one interacts on the basis of social identity group membership, one moves towards acting as a representative rather than as wholly independent. Here, depersonalisation moves the individual from being self-regulated in terms of behaviour to acting according to group norms. This is different from deindividuation in that depersonalisation does not imply a loss of rationality and civility in behaviour. The need to account for the presence of rationality in the group identity setting would become a central component of later criticism of deindividuation theory, as social identities can indeed exist simultaneously with individual identity, thus negating a complete loss of self (Reicher, 1987).

This dynamic is especially apparent in cases of conflict, where ideals clash and individuals interact based on group representations. Nowhere is this more apparent than in the message boards and comment sections of the Internet where heated arguments can appear among strangers in places having nothing to do with the topic of contention. The online setting truly offers a fresh glimpse into the dynamics of social identity processes: the comment section of a benign YouTube video can turn into a battlefield of philosophy, religion, politics or anything else for that matter.

Stereotyping and depersonalisation are centrally important to the dynamics of online hate, where categorisation and group norms work to damage a targeted group or individual. As individuals are grouped into negative categories, targets are no longer seen as unique individuals but rather as representatives of a hated group whose concept is driven by an oversimplified prototype. Skin colour, sexual orientation and religious belief are all examples of characteristics used to trigger hate despite the multitude of other characteristics held by the victims in question. A further danger of the group dynamic is that of shared responsibility. As depersonalisation takes place, harmful action can be justified by group norms rather than individual responsibility; a form of social anonymity emerges. Thus, social identity dynamics can magnify damage by encouraging extreme behaviours under the influence of a particular group.

This process of depersonalisation can produce all manner of perceptions, from greater empathy, mutual assistance and social acceptance, to deepened racism, ethnocentrism and sexism. Here, context is key; where validation and acceptance are found, so also is a set of norms whose adoption may be required for the continued meeting of social needs. If it is necessary to reinforce and to display harmful norms in order to maintain an affiliation, any mechanisms making that process easier or freer from possible accountability can facilitate great harm. It should be noted that this depersonalisation is a shift in self-concept and perception of others, and is not inherently damaging or beneficial. Rather, it

is the process by which social identity develops when adopting norms and representing an identity group one finds a connection with.

Experimenting with social identities is an important part of human development (Bosma & Kunnen, 2001; Cruwys, Haslam, Dingle, Haslam & Jetten,
2014; Gilman & Huebner, 2006). As individuals develop, particularly through
adolescence to emerging adulthood, they begin to question their place in
society, and consequently their identity and personal values (Arnett, 2004;
Erikson, 1963, 1980). For some, the Internet becomes a toy or virtual world for
escapism, while for others it is a learning tool or social instrument. Here, the
online setting is a tool for discovering one's identity through creating new areas
to explore while also facilitating contact with users unlike oneself (Liu, 2011).
Online, the interactional possibilities are endless, as are the identity groups to
which one has access. The potential for learning, entertainment and social fulfilment of the online setting is linked to the scale and accessibility of each.
Users who struggle with feelings of loneliness or social discomfort in school
tend to seek out interacting partners with whom they have no contact offline
(Livingstone, 2008). Online access enables the exploration of new contacts,
offering a validation that offline groups have not provided. Experimenting with
new identities and independent exploration of new aspects of the self have been
shown to be of great benefit to many users (Näsi, Räsäsen & Lehdonvirta,
2011). A multitude of individual needs for validation and group membership
are thereby met continually online.

Social media act as a tool here for relationship formation among users.
Finding group validation online creates a healthier state of mind in those
seeking support in various areas. Feeling understood and appreciated and
sharing significant interactions are especially strong predictors of wellbeing,
while their lack is a strong predictor of low self-esteem and depression (Reis,
Sheldon, Gable, Roscoe & Ryan, 2000). Indeed, Internet use is associated with
a decline in loneliness and with other positive social effects through the provision of beneficial social interaction and the discovery of identity groups. As
the Internet is more a facilitator than an inhibitor, its effects can be both beneficial and destructive, depending upon, fundamentally, the participant in question. This being the case, identity group cohesion can also be either destructive
or beneficial, the extent being determined by the group itself rather than the
dynamics common to both.

Group membership is a crucial component of the internal versus external nego-
tiation that is identity (Amiot, de la Sablionniere, Terry & Smith, 2007). As mentioned earlier, self-categorisation theory (Turner, 1985) suggests that identification
with any group is based on the extent to which individuals can enhance their social
identity through categorising themselves as group members (Chattopadhyay,
George & Lawrence, 2004). This theory proposes that individuals must associate
themselves and others with particular social categories to derive social identities,
often strengthened by identity prototypes or strong group norms (Turner, 1985).

Continual comparisons based on categorisation takes place within one's
social environment. One's environment is a determinant of what types of

comparison are possible. Online, the world is within users' reach, allowing them to contact any number of unique perspectives, backgrounds, motivations and interests. In this sense, the scope of identity development online is broadened due to the multiplicity of contacts and information sources. The link here between a broadened environment and identification processes is related to the previously mentioned risks and benefits available online. Just as the social aspects of the Internet can provide wonderful opportunities, so too can they reinforce harmful identifications.

Furthermore, the need for validation and social support sought online is especially prominent in users who are most actively seeking their place in the world (Livingstone, 2008). The customisation of one's social sphere is at a level never before seen, combined with all manner of self-validating online content suited to the demands of the user in question. Social media are full of fan clubs, support groups and interest-based communities of every shape and size. Here, users can become strongly bonded to online communities through shared goals or ideals. Notably, self-disclosure is a key component of relationship formation and maintenance as it fosters social trust both online and offline (Fogel & Nehmabd, 2009; Sheldon, 2009). Communication is a central component of bonding, also online. Regardless of the social disposition of a particular user, investment in online networks facilitates interpersonal trust, which is ultimately necessary for online communities to survive (Sheldon, 2009; Valenzuela, Park & Kee, 2009). As bonds are strengthened through shared interests and common goals or attitudes, users who trust are those who also remain committed to identity groups and especially prototypes.

Notably, the level of independence and individuality of a user is negatively related to the strength of identification with an online community or peer group and less autonomous users are therefore more likely to be strongly tied to online groups (Lehdonvirta & Räsänen, 2011). The implication for hate content online from these findings is one that adds to risk. Namely, impressionable users seeking validation and acceptance are most likely to bond with groups online, including ones espousing damaging values.

2.4 Social identity issues: online versus offline interaction

As social identity involves an overlap of internal and external processes, the Internet further enables users to develop and adopt multiple social identities and experiment with new virtual identities according to specific needs. Significantly, the Internet plays an important role in social identity formation and development as it allows individuals to explore values and beliefs within environments that they perceive to be relatively free from excessive external pressures.

A significant structural component of computer-mediated interaction inherent in most forms of communication online linked to relative safety through lessened visibility is modified social presence. In the online setting, the degree to which an interacting participant is experienced physically is typically diminished.

Whether chatting online with a friend, interacting on a comment section or message board through a username or customising a social media profile, users are typically interacting and presenting themselves in a less physically present manner. These different forms of social presence are essential to understanding the dynamics of online interaction. This modifier of social presence, or anonymity, is prevalent in various forms today and can be used for a number of purposes, whether beneficial or destructive.

Anonymity is an important aspect of the online setting and is best understood as a spectrum, ranging from less anonymous to more anonymous, that is, from visual anonymity to pseudonymity, then full anonymity (Keipi, 2015). This range of anonymity highlights some of the variation and dynamics of different online environments. Visual anonymity means that some user features are hidden, namely physical face-to-face characteristics. This form of anonymity has effects on disclosure and expression, even when users are otherwise known to one another (Joinson, 2001). Next, pseudonymity refers to navigation and interaction using created usernames or personas designed for the online setting which, despite being created for that setting, carry reputation effects. Finally, full anonymity means users are completely unknown and untraceable (Keipi & Oksanen, 2014); this is typically only feasible with the help of onion routers such as Tor.

In general terms, anonymity online carries two primary characteristics, namely diminished identifiability and diminished social presence, which can exist simultaneously or separately. A user is identifiable when their offline identity can be determined. Notably, social presence can be diminished even when users are known to one another. Users taking advantage of social media, for example, might be known to one another offline, yet social presence is absent in their communication and thus a degree of anonymity exists that may affect expression and disclosure (Keipi & Oksanen, 2014). Here, visibility is diminished despite the presence of identifiability. On the other hand, a user might participate in interaction using randomly generated video chat providers such as Omegle. Here, participants are visible but interaction is random and therefore not based on usernames. This would be an instance of high visibility but limited identifiability. Both of these components of online anonymity carry effects on interaction, especially in terms of disclosure.

Social trust is often a precondition of whether or not one wishes to remain anonymous or reveal one's identity in the online setting. Users who avoid face-to-face interaction are more likely to connect with others online, where some form of anonymity can be used to encourage self-disclosure (Merchant, 2012; Sheldon, 2008). Some degree of anonymity, namely being able to control the pace and type of information disclosed about oneself, one's physical appearance, and the ease of finding desired interactional partners based on traits, interests and predefined groups, makes an important difference between Internet communication and face-to-face interaction (Bargh & McKenna, 2004; Tanis & Postmes, 2007). Online, the capacity for avoiding unwanted physical reactions can encourage users to express themselves more openly due to lessened risk of a strong negative experience from the interacting partner while also increasing intimacy due to connecting on shared interests (Nowak, Watt & Walther, 2005; Qian & Scott, 2007).

The online setting and the way users can determine visibility affect some central dynamics of how interaction takes place. Emotional expression through facial features, for example, has been shown to be central in how reactions are formed and how responses are structured. Feedback is instantaneous, with non-verbal cues often transmitting reactions far more quickly and effectively than the spoken word or written text. Online, many of these cues are not available for users trying to determine the mindset of others with whom they are communicating. Interestingly, physical expression in the online setting is limited in the sense that live physical cues are typically missing, yet text and verbal communication may be enhanced. This is a unique new balance involving trading a great deal of the possibility to interpret others' immediate responses for an environment where one can express oneself more freely.

The anonymity of online interaction can provide a sense of safety for users and their social identity, allowing individuals to experiment with multiple identities online. Through various forms of social media, users are able to expand opportunities for identity exploration and self-validation. Virtual worlds, online chat sites, message boards and forums, social networking sites and content communities all provide unique ways of seeking out desired information or support. This evolution of online communities and social identity sources is made up of mechanisms and built-in interactional patterns that past interaction did not provide.

Linked to the anonymity available online is flexibility in terms of how one is viewed. Here, computer-mediated interaction combined with platforms of social media allow for a great deal of customisation in terms of how users wish to be viewed by interacting partners; self-presentation has become central to how users explore social opportunities online (Allen, Szwedo & Mikami, 2012). As mentioned, identifiability can be manipulated online, which may enhance both social benefits and individual exploration of identity, for example (Livingstone & Brake, 2010).

Much like the capacity for finding ideal online groups to match individual interests or values, the online setting allows for a significant degree of flexibility in terms of self-presentation in order to gain favour from desired audiences (Panek, Nardis & Konrath, 2013). Here, the possibility for desired peer recognition can be enhanced through controlling one's visible persona by producing an idealised self. Users thus have a multitude of options in this setting to enhance, diminish, create or ignore aspects of themselves that are perceived to influence a desired audience's attention. This idealised self can then be used to attract desired group membership (Anderson, Fagan, Woodnutt & Chamorro-Premuzic, 2012). Online, users can appear to be almost anyone, with specific interests, attitudes or characteristics brought to the forefront of their public profile. This flexibility is a particularly valuable tool when seeking out acceptance from a certain group revolving around a clear identity prototype, for example.

2.5 Social identity, Internet anonymity and online risk

The components of Social Identity Theory presented, namely self-presentation, self-categorisation and depersonalisation, are all central to a framework relevant to the dynamics of the online setting. Here, phenomena identified in the offline setting in terms of foundational social processes driving relational behaviour are applied to the online setting and its unique characteristics, combining the unique online environmental characteristic of anonymity with the inherent social identity processes carried by users.

Here, the Social Identity Model of Deindividuation Effects (SIDE) comes into play as an extension of Reicher's (1987) critique of deindividuation theory. SIDE, developed out of the aforementioned Social Identity Theory (Tajfel & Turner, 1986) and self-categorisation theory (Turner, 1982), was a wide-scale effort by Lea and Spears (1991) to reconcile various contradictory findings on the effects of anonymity. Before the SIDE model, as mentioned earlier, anonymity had been linked to all manner of behaviour, from increased aggression, deviance and dishonesty to increased empathy and cooperation. With SIDE, an effort was made to bring both positive and negative effects of anonymity into a common framework. This was carried out through experiments involving anonymity and computer-mediated communication in a laboratory setting. Participants' identity group membership was reinforced and interaction was studied in conditions of anonymity and identifiability. Results showed that anonymity combined with group membership increased conformity to group norms, thus establishing group self-awareness. This contradicts deindividuation theory which posits total loss of self-awareness. Here, the cognitive aspect of conforming to group norms was reinforced, as group ideals were embraced by anonymous participants even without group interaction or group control of behaviour in the experimental setting. Thus, conformity to the group was individually and therefore cognitively motivated even in conditions lacking group accountability.

SIDE thus proposes that as one interacts in conditions of social invisibility, or anonymity, there is a movement from thinking in terms of the self to thinking in terms of the group. This, as described earlier, is depersonalisation which comes about through the weakening of interpersonal cues of communication, causing a shift from self-awareness to group self-awareness by self-categorisation (Lea & Spears, 1995). This has the effect of promoting behaviour of the identity group that one bonds with without forcing a complete loss of self. Here, the complexity of the self is given up in favour of self-stereotyping in order to strengthen group bonds and better distinguish oneself from other groups.

Anonymity thus has the effect of influencing forms of self-categorisation and adherence to group norms as complex individuals are seen as simplified group representatives (Lea & Spears, 1991). This finding, in turn, helps to shed light on the dynamics of social interaction online by users in various states of anonymity. Online, especially through social media, common interests and aspects of personal identity can bind users to online communities with an enhanced effect.

This enhancement is rooted in connecting with other users on shared interests or identity characteristics in a more focused manner online, a process strengthened by a level of anonymity as users seek validation from a desirable target (Keipi & Oksanen, 2014). In the online setting, group identity dynamics tend to be enhanced during interaction where the filter of lessened identifiability or social presence can enhance certain identity characteristics as both participants become representatives of a given group. Figure 2.1 illustrates this phenomenon of depersonalisation, as the offline setting allows for more complete interaction in terms of physical cues. In the online setting, interaction is more focused, with narrower identity characteristics becoming visible between participants. Online, users meet on simplified grounds where things are dealt with and communicated in a contextually limited way. This limitation occurs both in terms of how one is perceived and how one sees the other.

The SIDE model linked to the aspects of social identity described earlier helps to explain why the comment section below an otherwise benign video or news article can turn into a warzone of politics, race or anything else. Here, social identity groups clash on the basis of stereotyping, seeing the "other" as an oversimplified representative of an opposing group. Though this process is common offline as well, the online setting includes a secondary mechanism,

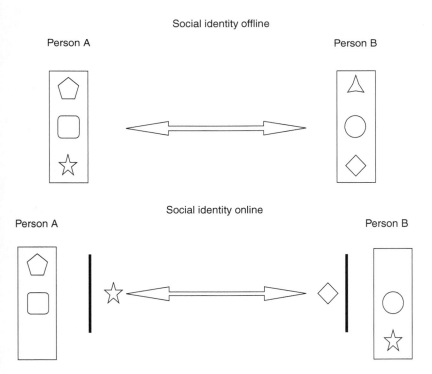

Figure 2.1 Online depersonalisation.

namely the aforementioned anonymity. This lessened social presence can, in turn, enhance stereotyping and group cohesion by limiting the visibility of the complex "other" while also potentially lessening the accountability of the users in question. Online, the dynamics of social identity and depersonalisation are similar to the offline setting, but online anonymity can magnify the limited view of the opposition in addition to further lessening the shared responsibility carried within a social identity group in the representative role.

These components of social identity formation, namely comparison, categorisation, norm reinforcement, prototype-based ideals and depersonalisation, are all prevalent online and help to explain highly popular behaviours there. The addition of lessened physical presence, customised self-presentation and access to wide audiences globally illuminates areas that go beyond the original offline social environment of SIT. These characteristics are particularly relevant in the weighing of online risk in terms of hate due to their applicability to harmful action. The identity reinforcement mechanisms available online are, in a number of the ways mentioned, enhanced compared to the offline space. Consequently, the targeting of others is also facilitated to a heightened degree. How does the online environment itself affect identity formation? Are there relevant structural components of the Internet that past theory does not account for due to its focus on the offline setting? Given the immense evolution in social interaction and the environments in which it occurs, it seems reasonable to suggest that a fresh look at how identity and risk intersect in the new online environment is warranted.

References

Abrams, D., & Hogg, M. (2004). Metatheory: Lessons from social identity research. *Personality and Social Psychology Review, 8*(2), 98–106. DOI: 10.1207/s15327957pspr0802_2.

Allen, J., Szwedo, D., & Mikami, A. (2012). Social networking site use predicts changes in young adults' psychological adjustment. *Journal of Research on Adolescence, 22,* 453–466. DOI: 10.1111/1532-7795.2012.00788.

Amiot, C. E., de la Sablonniere, R., Terry, D. J., & Smith, J. R. (2007). Integration of social identities in the self: Toward a cognitive-developmental model. *Personality and Social Psychology Review, 11*(4), 364–388. DOI: 10.1177/1088868307304091.

Anderson, B., Fagan, P., Woodnutt, T., & Chamorro-Premuzic, T. (2012). Facebook psychology: Popular questions answered by research. *Psychology of Popular Media Culture, 1*(1), 23–37. DOI: 10.1037/a0026452.

Arnett, J. J. (2004). *Emerging Adulthood: The Winding Road from the Late Teens Through the Twenties*. Oxford: Oxford University Press.

Bargh, J. A., & McKenna, K. Y. (2004). The Internet and social life. *Annual Review of Psychology, 55,* 573–590. DOI: 10.1146/annurev.psych.55.090902.141922.

Baumeister, R. F., & Leary, M. R. (1995). The need to belong: Desire for interpersonal attachments as a fundamental human motivation. *Psychological Bulletin, 117*(3), 497–529. DOI: 10.1037/0033-2909.117.3.497.

Billig, M. (2002). Henri Tajfel's "Cognitive aspects of prejudice" and the psychology of bigotry. *British Journal of Social Psychology, 41*(2), 171–188. DOI: 10.1348/0144666 02760060165.

Blais, J. J., Craig, W. M., Pepler, D., & Connolly, J. (2008). Adolescents online: The importance of Internet activity choices to salient relationships. *Journal of Youth and Adolescence, 37*(5), 522–536. DOI: 10.1007/s10964-007-9262-7.

Bosma, H. A., & Kunnen, E. S. (2001). Determinants and mechanisms in ego identity development: A review and synthesis. *Developmental Review, 21*(1), 39–66. DOI: 10.1006/drev.2000.0514.

Chattopadhyay, P., George, E., & Lawrence, S. A. (2004). Why does dissimilarity matter? Exploring self-categorisation, self-enhancement, and uncertainty reduction. *Journal of Applied Psychology, 89*(5), 892–900. DOI: 10.1037/0021-9010.89.5.892.

Cruwys, T., Haslam, S. A., Dingle, G. A., Haslam, C., & Jetten, J. (2014). Depression and social identity: An integrative review. *Personality and Social Psychology Review, 18*(3), 215–238. DOI: 10.1177/1088868314523839.

Davidson, J., & Martelozzo, E. (2013). Exploring young people's use of social networking sites and digital media in the Internet safety context. *Information, Communication & Society, 16*(19), 1456–1476. DOI: 10.1080/1369118X.2012.701655.

Diener, E. (1979). Deindividuation, self-awareness, and disinhibition. *Journal of Personality and Social Psychology, 37*(7), 1160–1171. DOI: 10.1037/0022-3514.37.7.1160.

Erikson, E. H. (1963). *Childhood and Society* (2nd edn). New York: Norton.

Erikson, E. H. (1980). *Identity and the Life Cycle*. New York: Norton.

Festl, R., & Quandt, T. (2013). Social relations and cyberbullying: The influence of individual and structural attributes on victimisation and perpetration via the Internet. *Human Communication Research, 39*(1), 101–126. DOI: 10.1111/j.1468-2958.2012.01442.x.

Fogel, J., & Nehmadb, E. (2009). Internet social networking communities: Risk taking, trust, and privacy concerns. *Computers in Human Behaviour, 25*, 153–160. DOI: 10.1016/j.chb.2008.08.006.

Gergen, K. J., Gergen, M. M., & Barton, W. H. (1973). Deviance in the dark. *Psychology Today, 7*(5), 129–130. Retrieved from www.swarthmore.edu/Documents/faculty/gergen/Deviance_in_the_dark.pdf.

Gilman, R., & Huebner, E. (2006). Characteristics of adolescents who report very high life satisfaction. *Journal of Youth and Adolescence, 35*(3), 293–301. DOI: 10.1007/s10964-006-9036-7.

Hogan, B. (2010). The presentation of self in the age of social media: Distinguishing performances and exhibitions online. *Bulletin of Science Technology & Society, 30*(6), 377–386. DOI: 10.1177/0270467610385893.

Hogg, M. A., & Terry, D. (2001). *Attitudes, Behaviour and Social Context*. Philadelphia, PA: Psychology Press.

Hogg, M. A., Terry, D. J., & White, K. M. (1995). A tale of two theories: A critical comparison of identity theory with social identity theory. *Social Psychology Quarterly, 58*(4), 255–269. DOI: 10.2307/2787127.

Jenkins, R. (2004). *Social Identity*. London: Routledge.

Johnson, R. D., & Downing, L. L. (1979). Deindividuation and valence of cues: Effects on prosocial and antisocial behavior. *Journal of Personality and Social Psychology, 37*(9), 1532–1538. DOI: 10.1037/0022-3514.37.9.1532.

Joinson, A. (2001). Self-disclosure in computer-mediated communication: The role of self-awareness and visual anonymity. *European Journal of Social Psychology, 31*, 177–192. DOI: 10.1002/ejsp. 36.

Keipi, T. (2015). Now you see me, now you don't: A study of the relationship between Internet anonymity and Finnish young people (Doctoral dissertation). Retrieved from: www.doria.fi/handle/10024/113050.

Keipi, T., & Oksanen, A. (2014). Self-exploration, anonymity and risks in the online setting: Analysis of narratives by 14–18-year olds. *Journal of Youth Studies, 17*, 1097–1113. DOI: 10.1080/13676261.2014.881988.

Lea, M., & Spears, R. (1991). Computer-mediated communication, de-individuation and group decision-making. *International Journal of Man-Machine Studies, 34*(2), 283–301. DOI: 10.1016/0020-7373(91)90045-9.

Lea, M., & Spears, R. (1995). Love at first byte? Building personal relationships over computer networks. In J. Wood & S. Duck (Eds.), *Understudied Relationships: Off the Beaten Track*. Thousand Oaks, CA: Sage.

Lehdonvirta, V., & Räsänen, P. (2011). How do young people identify with online and offline peer groups? A comparison between UK, Spain, and Japan. *Journal of Youth Studies, 14*(1), 91–108. DOI: 10.1080/13676261.2010.506530.

Liu, F. (2011). Wired for fun: Narratives by members of China's E-generation. *Young, 19*, 69–89. DOI: 10.1177/110330881001900105.

Livingstone, S. (2008). Taking risky opportunities in youthful content creation: Teenagers' use of social networking for intimacy, privacy, and self-expression. *New Media & Society, 10*(3), 393–411. DOI: 10.1177/1461444808089415.

Livingstone, S., & Brake, D. (2010). On the rapid rise of social networking sites: New findings and policy implications. *Children & Society, 24*(1), 75–83. DOI: 10.1111/j.1099-0860.2009.00243.x.

Matheson, K., & Zanna, M. P. (1988). The impact of computer-mediated communication on self-awareness. *Computers in Human Behavior, 4*(3), 221–233. DOI: 10.1016/0747-5632(88)90015-5.

Merchant, G. (2012). Unraveling the social network: Theory and research. *Learning, Media & Technology, 37*(1), 4–19. DOI: 10.1080/17439884.2011.567992.

Näsi, M., Räsänen, P., & Lehdonvirta, V. (2011). Identification with online and offline communities: Understanding ICT disparities in Finland. *Technology in Society, 33*(1–2), 4–11. DOI: 10.1016/j.techsoc.2011.03.003.

Näsi, M., Räsänen, P., Oksanen, A., Hawdon, J., Keipi, T., & Holkeri, E. (2014). Association between online harassment and exposure to harmful online content: A cross-national comparison between the United States and Finland. *Computers in Human Behaviour, 41*, 137–145. DOI: 10.1016/j.chb.2014.09.019.

Nowak, K., Watt, J., & Walther, J. (2005). The influence of synchrony and sensory modality on the person perception process in computer-mediated groups. *Journal of Computer-Mediated Communication, 10*(3), article 3. DOI: 10.1111/j.1083-6101.2005.tb00251.x.

Oksanen, A., & Keipi, T. (2013). Young people as victims of crime on the Internet: A population-based study in Finland. *Vulnerable Children and Youth Studies, 8*(4), 298–309. DOI: 10.1080/17450128.2012.752119.

Oksanen, A., Hawdon, J., & Räsänen, P. (2014). Glamorising rampage online: School shooting fan communities on YouTube. *Technology in Society, 39*, 55–67. DOI: 10.1016/j.techsoc.2014.08.001.

Oksanen, A., Hawdon, J., Holkeri, E., Näsi, M., & Räsänen, P. (2014). Exposure to online hate among young social media users. *Sociological Studies of Children & Youth, 18*, 253–273. DOI: 10.1108/S1537-466120140000018021.

Panek, E., Nardis, Y., & Konrath, S. (2013). Mirror or megaphone? How relationships between narcissism and social networking site use differ on Facebook and Twitter. *Computers in Human Behaviour, 29*(5), 2004–2012. DOI: 10.1016/j.chb.2013.04.012.

Qian, H., & Scott, C. (2007). Anonymity and self-disclosure on weblogs. *Journal of Computer-Mediated Communication, 12*(4), 1428–1451. DOI: 10.1111/j.1083-6101. 2007.00380.x.

Reicher, S. D. (1987). Crowd behaviour as social action. In J. C. Turner, M. A. Hogg, P. J. Oakes, S. D. Reicher & M. S. Wetherell (Eds.), *Rediscovering the Social Group: A Self-Categorisation Theory* (pp. 171–202). Oxford: Basil Blackwell.

Reis, H. T., Sheldon, K. M., Gable, S. L., Roscoe, J., & Ryan, R. M. (2000). Daily well-being: The role of autonomy, competence, and relatedness. *Personality and Social Psychology Bulletin, 26*(4), 419–435. DOI: 10.1177/0146167200266002.

Sheldon, P. (2008). The relationship between unwillingness to communicate and students' Facebook use. *Journal of Media Psychology, 20*, 67–75. DOI: 10.1027/1864-1105.20.2.67.

Sheldon, P. (2009). I'll poke you. You'll poke me! Self-disclosure, social attraction, predictability and trust as important predictors of Facebook relationships. *Cyberpsychology: Journal of Psychosocial Research on Cyberspace, 3*(2), article 1. Retrieved from http://cyberpsychology.eu/view.php?cisloclanku=2009111101&article=(search in Issues).

Singer, J. E., Brush, C. A., & Lublin, S. C. (1965). Some aspects of deindividuation: Identification and conformity. *Journal of Experimental Social Psychology, 1*(4), 356–378. DOI: 10.1016/0022-1031(65)90015-6.

Tajfel, H. (1972). Experiments in a vacuum. In J. Israel & H. Tajfel (Eds.), *The Context of Social Psychology: A Critical Assessment* (pp. 69–119). Oxford, England: Academic Press.

Tajfel, H. (1974). Social identity and intergroup behaviour. *Social Science Information/ sur les sciences sociales, 13*(2), 65–93. DOI: 10.1177/053901847401300204.

Tajfel, H. (1979). Individuals and groups in social psychology. *British Journal of Social and Clinical Psychology, 18*(2), 183–190.DOI: 10.1111/j.2044-8260.1979.tb00324.x.

Tajfel, H. (1981). *Human Groups and Social Categories: Studies in Social Psychology.* Cambridge: CUP Archive. DOI: 10.1177/053901847401300204.

Tajfel, H., & Turner, J. C. (1979). An integrative theory of intergroup conflict. *The Social Psychology of Intergroup Relations, 33*(47), 74.

Tajfel, H. & Turner, J. (1986). The social identity theory of intergroup behaviour. In S. Worchel & W. Austin (Eds.), *Psychology of Intergroup Relations* (pp. 7–24). Chicago, IL: Nelson-Hall.

Tanis, M., & Postmes, T. (2007). Two faces of anonymity: Paradoxical effects of cues to identity in CMC. *Computers in Human Behaviour, 23*(2), 955–970. DOI: 10.1016/j. chb.2005.08.004.

Thoits, P. A., Virshup, L. K., Lauren, K., & Ashmore, R. (1997). Me's and we's: Forms and functions of social identities. In J. Lee (Ed.), *Self and Identity: Fundamental Issues* (pp. 106–133). New York: Oxford University Press.

Turner, J. C. (1975). Social comparison and social identity: Some prospects for intergroup behaviour. *European Journal of Social Psychology, 5*(1), 1–34. DOI: 10.1002/ejsp. 2420050102.

Turner, J. C. (1982). Towards a cognitive redefinition of the social group. *Current Psychology of Cognition, 1*(2), 93–118.

Turner, J. C. (1985). Social categorisation and the self-concept: A social cognitive theory of group behaviour. In E. J. Lawler (Ed.), *Advances in Group Processes* (pp. 77–122). Greenwich, CT: JAI Press.

Turner, J. C. & Brown, R. J. (1978). Social status, cognitive alternatives and intergroup relations. In H. Tajfel (Ed.), *Differentiation between Social Groups* (pp. 201–234). London: Academic Press.

Turner, J. C. & Reynolds, K. J. (2010). The story of social identity. In T. Postmes & N. R. Branscomber (Eds.), *Rediscovering Social Identity: Key Readings* (pp. 13–32). New York: Psychology Press.

Valenzuela, S., Park, N., & Kee, K. (2009). Is there social capital in a social network site? Facebook use and college students' life satisfaction, trust, and participation. *Journal of Computer-Mediated Communication, 14*(4), 875–901. DOI: 10.1111/j.1083-6101. 2009.01474.x.

Walther, J. (1996). Computer-mediated communication: Impersonal, interpersonal, and hyperpersonal interaction. *Communication Research, 23*(1), 3–43. DOI: 10.1177/ 009365096023001001.

Wang, S., & Stefanone, M. (2013). Showing off? Human mobility and the interplay of traits, self-disclosure, and Facebook check-ins. *Social Science Computer Review, 31*, 437–457. DOI: 10.1177/0894439313481424.

Wegge, D., Vandebosch, H., Eggermont, S., & Walrave, M. (2015). The strong, the weak, and the unbalanced the link between tie strength and cyberaggression on a social network site. *Social Science Computer Review, 33*(3), 315–342. DOI: 10.1177/ 0894439314546729.

Zimbardo, P. (1969). The human choice: Individuation, reason, and order vs. deindividuation, impulse and chaos. In W. Arnold & D. Levine (Eds.), *Nebraska Symposium on Motivation, 17*, 237–307. Lincoln: University of Nebraska Press.

3   Lifestyle and online risks

3.1 The conditions of risk

Risk of varying degrees is a normal part of everyday life. Daily routines can
carry the potential for a negative or less than ideal outcome; traffic delays may
cause problems at school or at work, weather conditions may change suddenly,
resulting in inconvenience in terms of plans, and individual choices can affect
the outcome of one's routine in any number of slightly or extremely harmful
ways. In the offline setting, risks tend to involve physical space, driven by some
level of face-to-face interaction and consequence of choices or circumstance.
Here, damage resulting from risk comes as an extension of the situation to which
an individual has been exposed.

Past experience and advice from trusted others in general help us to navigate
through various forms of risk. We all take regular steps daily to ensure positive
outcomes in practical ways. Avoiding or minimising potential risk may be as
simple as locking one's car doors, avoiding specific city streets after a certain
time of day, or checking the weather forecast before making travel plans. Some
leave the lights on at home when travelling, keep valuables hidden when walking
through high-crime areas, or avoid sharing credit card information where trans-
actions seem unsafe. However, avoiding risk is not always simply an issue of
modifying behaviour to pre-empt harm. Even when routines and regular environments are relatively free from the likelihood of high risk, other key factors can
intrude, regardless of perceptions of safety.

The choices of other independent actors with whom one comes into contact
either directly or indirectly are a central source of risk and therefore also of victimisation. A choice to steal, cheat or attack can have nothing to do with the
actions of the victim apart from being physically present or randomly exposed
by unrelated choices. The likelihood of victimisation is not a simple thing to cal-
culate when the potential intent of others seeking to harm cannot be known.
Though some measure of safety can be ensured by limiting one's exposure to
people, places and environmental conditions, risks can find their targets when
victims are accessible and aggressors are mobile and motivated. The level of
social risk can be hard to predict owing to the difficulty of predicting the choices
and motivations of others. Sharing the same physical space with dangerous

individuals is an obvious source of heightened risk, regardless of how benign a potential victim's behaviour may be.

Thus, we all carry notions of what qualify as high-risk individuals, places, times and locations. Regardless of routine or lifestyle, an awareness of what is possible in a negative sense is present offline. But the components of prevention capacity, victim accessibility and aggressor choice are all relevant to the online setting as well despite, the lack of physical presence. Therefore, in continuing the theoretical discussion of the previous chapter, the transition to the online setting with its unique characteristics illustrates the need to contextualise the social aspects of the Internet in terms of risk. This is central to an assessment of hate online, as it occurs in a certain social space with unique mechanisms of communication, access to others and content creation. As the study of offline risk has been around far longer than research on online risk, a good understanding of online victimisation requires a look at past theoretical frameworks connected to assessing victimisation.

When discussing risk, it is helpful to distinguish between absolute and probabilistic exposure. These two work together to determine the general likelihood of victimisation. Here, absolute exposure involves those people, places, times or materials that are prerequisites for a given form of victimisation. For example, inaccessible victims make targeting impossible just as a lack of material goods makes theft of those goods impossible. Victimisation cannot therefore occur without absolute exposure, namely contact between aggressor and victim. Absolute exposure is a prerequisite for probabilistic exposure. If homes are available to be robbed, then differences between experiences of theft victimisation among a population become possible. This probability refers to the likelihood of negative experience in terms of certain people, places or times, for example. Different activities, routines, social environments and attitudes carry unique levels of risk compared to otherwise equivalent others; some city streets are more dangerous than others, some deviant behaviours are more severely penalised and some interactions are more likely to result in personal harm.

3.2 Starting points for understanding victimisation

In past research on risk assessment, environmental factors have been central, namely through an identification of key issues contributing to dangerous or harmful interactions. The environments in which a person can be victimised today have widened in scope with the introduction of Internet-based communication. The sphere of influence of users and the potential sources of negative experience have grown exponentially. Traditional settings for victimisation, such as homes, city streets and workplaces, have been extended to the non-tangible and globally accessible online environment in devices carried in users' pockets throughout their everyday lives.

Just as in the offline setting, individuals use the online space to perform certain routines, for example checking emails and certain social media profiles on a daily basis. However, users also encounter online material accidentally, becoming lost in the interconnections of the web, entering websites they did not intend to visit, being exposed to hostility, and experiencing victimisation. Here, users' online lifestyles affect online victimisation just as offline lifestyles affect offline victimisation. However, despite the extensive use of the online space for exploration and socialising, as well as the growing body of literature investigating online victimisation, it is not particularly clear who is most at risk of being victimised in the virtual world, who is not, and why that is.

The online setting and the hardware facilitating its use have radically transformed communication and access to others over the past few decades. Interaction is instant without being tied to a shared physical space. Mobile devices are continually present in daily life, acting as a window into the content and users of a global marketplace. Indeed, the benefits of this interactive landscape are vast, but what about the risks? Has the risk environment changed with the move to the online setting?

Early approaches to understanding victimisation through systemic theory include Lifestyle-Exposure Theory (LET) (Hindelang, Gottfredson & Garofalo, 1978) and Routine Activity Theory (RAT) (Cohen & Felson, 1979), which have come to form a foundation of research and victimisation. Both of these frameworks are concerned with understanding the ways in which patterns of lifestyles and routine activities in the social context allow various forms of victimisation, with LET providing a broader probabilistic view and RAT a more focused situational one built around the convergence of three factors, namely a motivated offender, a suitable target and a lack of capable guardians. According to RAT and LET, the combination of these three factors results in victimisation. Both theories emphasise that the point of aggressor opportunity is determined in large part by the activity patterns of daily life (Cohen, 1981). Here, negative experience is linked to the ways in which the individual in question carries out routine activities.

LET and RAT have much in common through overlapping themes and terminology, and this has led to them being paired together in past research. Their similarities have encouraged researchers to use them together and even interchangeably (e.g. Stewart, Elifson & Sterk, 2004; Wilcox, Sullivan, Jones & Van Gelder, 2014). Both are concerned with victimisation that occurs through a convergence of a motivated offender, an attractive target and the absence of a capable guardian, yet they approach risk in different ways. Furthermore, both theories share the same core terminology, with LET's Hindelang and colleagues (1978) coining the term "routine activities", which would later be taken up by RAT's Cohen and Felson (1979).

In terms of past implementation, LET has been less prominent in research and testing despite its prominence in setting the stage for understanding risk and the development of other theoretical approaches (Holt & Bossler, 2008; Meier & Miethe, 1993). Its contributions focus on the contextual factors that help to determine susceptibility to risk through various demographic measures that are themselves tied to the central role of lifestyles involving various degrees of risk. Furthermore, its take on the risk context is valuable in setting the stage for more focused and tested approaches. RAT, on the other hand, has been a central component in various approaches to victimisation research. We will first provide a discussion of the fundamentals of LET in order to create a helpful context for a closer look at RAT in order to apply it more specifically to the topic of online hate which is so central here.

LET represents one of the earliest systemic theories concerned with victimisation. Originally, Hindelang et al. (1978) developed the framework in order to deepen understanding of differences in the risks of victimisation across various social groups. Here demographic differences in the likelihood of being victimised are linked to variance in the lifestyle choices of victims. According to LET, these differences are significant due to their being linked to various risk levels in individuals, groups and places, for example. With certain combinations of lifestyle factors come situations of heightened risk of victimisation. It is clear that living in high-crime areas raises the likelihood of victimisation above that in rural locations where potential threats are limited due to a limited number of aggressors. The contextual factors related to individual exposure are central here, through identifying characteristics that can be linked to various social dangers.

Demographic factors can reflect the conditions of daily life, and can be useful in mapping the likelihood of experiencing risk situations. As mentioned earlier, risk is a part of daily life to varying degrees across populations. Depending on individual behaviour and social context, experience of risk may be unexpected in one setting and unsurprising in another. Here, high-volume activities may naturally predispose individuals to risk or help to prevent victimisation. Where contact with others, including potential offenders, is higher, so is the likelihood of facing danger of some degree. It follows that spending time at home is negatively related to victimisation, while time spent in public settings opens the door to all manner of risk. This is unsurprising, given that the prerequisites for aggression are less commonly present in the homes of victims than in more public settings where access, escape and target value are generally found.

Although Hindelang and colleagues (1978) used demographic characteristics including age, gender and race in the analysis of risk, they were primarily concerned with how likely victimisation is for those who share certain traits. It is important to note that lifestyles are central to LET, although individual traits are used to help identify certain behavioural trends (Pratt & Turanovic, 2016). This progression leads to the conclusion that young men are assumed to have lifestyles quite different from those of elderly women. Furthermore, LET maintains that lifestyle characteristics or norms that contribute to the likelihood of risk are socially determined by structural constraints, collective responses and role expectations. Group dynamics are thus highly relevant here in terms of determining lifestyle differences. Thus, the characteristics that make certain lifestyles distinct are important as markers of shared expectations concerning behavioural norms and the structural factors that act to either limit or enable available behavioural choices. As one lives one's daily life adhering to certain structural or social expectations, LET argues that patterns of activities emerge along with reinforcing associations that contextualise one's social environment. Taken a step further, these patterns of behaviour, or lifestyles, along with the corresponding associations, can either reinforce or diminish the likelihood of victimisation through affecting levels of vulnerability and levels of contact with various sources of risk.

These contextual elements of victimisation theory provided by LET act as a baseline here for RAT, which is concerned with the links between routines and risk exposure. For our purposes here the contributions of LET are used to set the theoretical stage in terms of risk for the more widely tested RAT. We therefore transition from the probabilistic lifestyle characteristics approach to more focused behavioural or situational factors associated with the patterns of individuals that are linked to victimisation. In doing this, we build on LET by delving into RAT and link this past research to the unique and often risk-enhancing characteristics fostered by the online environment. This, in turn, helps to clarify certain key limitations inherent in past victimisation theory when applied to the evolving social setting available online.

According to RAT, everyday routines place individuals at risk of victimisation by exposing them to dangerous people, places and situations. Thus crime can occur when a motivated offender, a suitable target and a lack of capable guardians are present simultaneously. Here, the convergence of these three components determines the occurrence of an experience of victimisation. As a theoretical tool, RAT has been well established and much used for the study of various forms of aggressor behaviour resulting in victimisation. Its framework is also concise and highly applicable to a diverse set of environments and situations. It has therefore been widely used in offline victimisation research (e.g. Stewart et al., 2004; Tewksbury & Mustaine, 2000). The framework maintains that four components are central to the process of victimisation, namely the issues of value, inertia, visibility and accessibility. First, in terms of value, the offender weighs the value of the fulfilment resulting from targeting a victim. This could be an issue of gratifying aggressive tendencies or simply the monetary value from a robbery. Second, as regarding inertia, the offender measures the level of resistance that the target is able to offer. A ready defence or difficulty in achieving the aggressor's goal is a strong deterrent. Third, in terms of visibility, a target must be identifiable by the offender in order to be targeted. Here, the degree to which the aggressor' is aware of suitable targets helps to determine the viability of negative action. Finally, in the case of accessibility, the offender is concerned with the possibility of escape, once targeting is complete. If it is very difficult to avoid identification, the offender will be motivated to avoid action.

Thus, routine activities in which people engage can become risky environments where being a target is determined by exposure to dangerous people, places and situations, and is influenced by the ability of potential guardians to confront potential offenders. RAT argues that if individuals' routines expose them to potential offenders in unguarded environments, criminal victimisation will occur (Felson & Boba, 2010; Reyns, Henson & Fisher, 2011). Specifically, the greater the exposure and proximity to motivated offenders and attractive targets, the greater the number of instances of victimisation. Conversely, guardianship protects against victimisation by discouraging harmful activity.

3.3 A comparison of LET and RAT

Despite their similarities, there is a key difference between LET's and RAT's frameworks in terms of how the risk of victimisation is approached, one that Pratt and Turanovic (2016) argue has been forgotten in much practical application of the theories. Namely, LET focuses on exposure to high-risk places, people and times where risk and victimisation are seen as a function of probability. Being involved in behaviours one might consider risky such as theft or drug use does not ensure victimisation, but taking part in such things does increase its likelihood. On the other hand, RAT is focused on the convergence of targets and offenders in a shared time and space where guardians are not present as determining victimisation in absolute terms.

RAT proposes that the absence of any of the three components (motivated offender, suitable target, lack of guardianship) is enough to prevent crimes involving victimisation. Probability of risk is therefore not the focus here, but rather a description of the victimisation as it unfolds (Pratt & Turanovic, 2016). This lack of emphasis on probabilistic risk was taken further by Cohen and Felson (1979) to show that risk is connected not only to risky routines but also to everyday activities. Central to their early theory was the argument that victimisation is not necessarily a result of relative deprivation during difficult economic times. Rather, times of prosperity could mean more theft as there is more to steal. Thus, risk of victimisation through theft was seen to be possible when families left home to carry out everyday routines that would leave their homes vulnerable to theft due to lack of guardianship. Here, targets, motivated offenders and a lack of guardianship converge as a result of routines that limit the victim's ability to prevent harmful action.

Certain routines are riskier than others and thus more liable to facilitate victimisation. That is the territory of LET, focused on the probability of risk. RAT's original focus on the risks of leaving the home vulnerable must be kept in mind when the framework is used to assess risky routines. RAT is concerned with the presence of three structural components of risk and victimisation, while LET takes account of the presence of varying degrees of these components in various settings resulting in a probabilistic point of view.

For both, physical proximity to high-risk environments plays a central role in experiences of victimisation. As the space between potential targets and aggressors increases, the role of proximity as a deterrent to negative experience is clear; much risk is avoided when potentially damaging interactions are physically impossible. It is intuitive that spending significant amounts of time in high-crime areas means higher levels of potential interaction with aggressors who have given those places their negative reputation, thus increasing the risk of becoming a victim. If time is spent where many aggressors are most comfortable, the cost of committing aggressive acts is lessened (Cohen, Kluegel & Land, 1981). This is particularly evident in, for example, perceptions of the dangers of inner-city areas where violence and aggression may be more likely. Here, perceived vulnerability is attributed to degree of proximity according to both LET, in terms of probability, and RAT, in absolute terms of whether the three components converge.

Furthermore, risks of personal victimisation are a function of the amount of time spent in public places in general, especially during times when darkness can be exploited to lessen the identifiability of the aggressor (Hindelang et al., 1978). Here, settings where lots of interaction is possible, access to potential victims is high and accountability can be manipulated, become high-risk environments. As such, public spaces prove helpful to aggressors in a number of ways. First, one need not justify one's presence there and thus searching for victims can be explained by any number of reasons; there is no cost of entry into such a space, and inclusion is not predicated on any enforced criteria. Open spaces are available to all, regardless of qualification or intent.

Furthermore, the visibility of targets is central to determining whether a motivated offender takes action. Assessing target suitability involves a series of steps. First, it must be possible to identify a suitable victim, whose individual characteristics are deemed minimally risky if the negative action is taken. Second, the target must be accessible to the aggressor. Simply identifying a target does not cause any damage to that target if further action is not possible due to physical constraints or protection mechanisms, for example. Third, a target is determined to be suitable if it is attractive to the offender, whether in terms of symbolic or economic value. In terms of common theft, easily transportable items with high value are ideal targets due to high reward combined with easy concealment of the targeted item and therefore of the role of the aggressor who would otherwise be liable for punishment.

3.4 Theoretical gaps in Internet research

We have entered a new online interactional space globally, and frameworks of risk invariably change with the environment. The basic premises of RAT and LET involving a convergence of victim and aggressor in time and physical space change if the setting is non-physical. Although there exists no new, widely tested theoretical risk framework for the online setting, RAT has been applied to various Internet-based phenomena. Early applications of RAT to the online setting were therefore focused on experiences of victimisation (Choi, 2008), cyberbullying (Holt & Bossler, 2008), Internet fraud (Pratt, Holtfreter & Reisig, 2010) and cyberattacks through viruses and information theft (Kigerl, 2011), for example. Here, users' actions created target suitability, with high levels of online activity being directly linked to victimisation and targeting in these areas. More recently, RAT has also been applied to online issues including overall cybercrime experiences (Näsi, Oksanen, Keipi & Räsänen, 2015), hacking (Leukfeldt, 2014), harassment (van Wilsem, 2013), unwanted sexual attention

(Holt, Bossler, Malinski & May, 2016), cyberstalking (Reyns, Henson & Fisher, 2015) and a combination of hacking, malware, identity theft, consumer fraud and stalking (Leukfeldt & Yar, 2016).

Furthermore, the general approach of LET and RAT to linking time spent in public spaces to risk has a parallel in the online setting. Here, targets' accessibility to motivated offenders has been shown to lead to victimisation through direct user-to-user messaging (e.g., Holt et al., 2016; Mitchell, Finkelhor, Jones & Wolak, 2010) and social media use (e.g. Holt, Fitzgerald, Bossler, Chee & Ng, 2015; Marcum, Higgins & Ricketts, 2010; Mitchell, Jones, Finkelhor & Wolak, 2013). Despite the applicability of RAT online, certain characteristics of offline theory are of doubtful relevance to the online setting due to fundamental differences in how interaction and navigation take place.

The central question here is to what extent the theoretical concepts developed for the offline setting can be effectively used to study behaviour in the online environment. Indeed, RAT's applicability online is contentious. On one hand, online victimisation is regarded as a new phenomenon due to the novelty of the environment in which it takes place while, on the other hand, RAT is viewed as perfectly applicable due to its provision of adequate means for assessing occurrences of victimisation (Leukfeldt & Yar, 2016). Again, the risk involved in spending time in a given environment is a product of how motivated an offender is, how accessible a victim is, and how protected that victim is externally. However, applying RAT to the online risk environment rather than to typical settings prevalent offline can be problematic due to fundamental differences between the two social environments that diminish the relevance of key risk pillars of the theory (Marcum et al., 2010; Reyns, 2013; Yar, 2005).

In the study of risks associated with routine activities, social situations mediate the likelihood of an individual or group taking an action that is harmful to others. Offline, according to RAT, situations where damaging action is determined to be effective depend on a particular convergence in the same physical space at the same time. Without this convergence of target and offender, victimisation is unlikely. The online setting presents an interesting alternative environment. Here, routines certainly exist but the dynamics of convergence are different. Online, a multitude of global users are constantly available for interaction or communication. Convergence is possible on a level never before seen, affording a great deal of opportunity for potential offenders. This convergence is no longer physical, which is central to RAT, but rather social or content-driven. The online setting is also less ordered in the sense that routines of offenders, victims and guardians rarely coincide in physical space and identifying patterns of this convergence is particularly challenging online. As such, the social space provided by the Internet goes far beyond the limits of offline spheres of influence in terms of factors contributing to risk. Figure 3.1 illustrates changes in the three key components of RAT between the online and offline settings.

Online, the incentives driving aggressors are also potentially different from the offline setting in that physical gratification is rarely sought. Rather, online

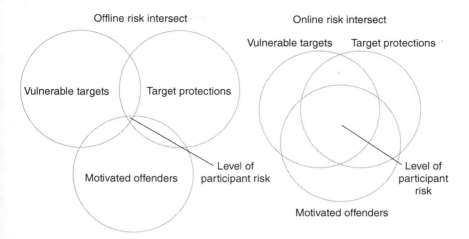

Figure 3.1 Routine activity risk online and offline.

[handwritten: online]

hate targeting is driven more by intangible motivations that can take many forms. Here, damaging targeting can take place in a shared online space and time or in settings determined by users unknown to the aggressor later on due to material remaining accessible beyond the creator's intended target and location online. The online marketplace for this sort of gratification is immense, as targets abound, identifiability can be limited, access to escape is convenient and targets are vulnerable to abuse. Compared to the offline setting, online aggressors, are at a great advantage when carrying out their targeting. Anonymity can be used to disguise identity and help in escaping from a situation, the convenience of navigation in social media platforms allows for efficient movement between interactional locations, and a huge number of suitable targets are easily searchable by identifying characteristics or social profiles online. *[handwritten margin: Anonymity online foils aggressor]*

Furthermore, the number of motivated offenders is exponentially greater than those of any one given city, no matter how large a population it holds. Second, online users are highly accessible in most social media. Interests, social identity groups and self-presented characteristics are often clearly visible on the Internet's social platforms. Finally, user protections online are limited due to the scope and ease of access to others and various forms of content. Exposure to harmful content or specific targeting can even be accidental online, where negative material is not necessarily categorised as such and kept separate from other content within social media platforms. Offline victimisation theory provides a framework in which online harassment, bullying and hate should be included as they constitute cases of externally imposed harm. Thus, although the online environment may be different from the offline, the mechanisms and interactional characteristics remain equivalent, even if enhanced and linked to lessened social presence that eliminates the necessity for physical convergence. *[handwritten margin: ① more aggressors ② users more accessible ③ protection limited due to ease of info]*

[handwritten at bottom: → environs diff – enhanced – not linked to social presence. not req. social convergence]

The environmental aspect of anonymity online also adds to the negative aspects of user experience in terms of risk through enabling aggressors in new ways. As users have recourse to easier forms of self-concealment, the external costs of aggression can be lessened (Keipi & Oksanen, 2014). This is especially closely linked to the visibility and accessibility components of RAT. Namely, anonymity can be used to manage visibility in order to lessen accountability that might otherwise result from targeted victimisation. Also, anonymity can be leveraged to create a customised self that can then be used to gain access to victims who might otherwise avoid contact with the aggressor. Notably, anonymity is beneficial to the aggressor not only in direct interaction but also in terms of creation of content whose second- and third-degree effects may be felt in perpetuity by unsuspecting users who encounter various forms of damaging material, even if the original intent was not to target them specifically. Here, the scope of sources of victimisation is broadened by the combination of content permanence and heightened negative expression as a result of the use of pseudonyms, for example.

Thus, the components and prerequisites of RAT benefit from an environmental update in terms of how the online setting differs. First, convergence in physical space is now less relevant to the experience of victimisation as aggressive interactions are carried out in a shared platform or social network. Furthermore, temporal convergence can also be irrelevant, as content created to target others can be easily accessed accidentally, resulting in damage from exposure. Thus the two prerequisites for victimisation to occur are expanded in that convergence is virtual and an ever present possibility whenever one navigates online. Here, the victimisation results from content created by another user, and its negative effects need not be tied to shared time and space. The issue of guardianship is also altered, as online co-presence at the moment of interaction or exposure to the content concerned cannot prevent the expression of hate by an aggressor. Instead, software providing various filters, firewalls and navigation controls may detect risk though these protections are far from comprehensive.

Here, in terms of RAT especially, the foundational assumption that regular routines can involve risk where the three primary factors converge is affected. LET's core of lifestyle factors based on behavioural patterns that involve risk and stem partly from victim choices are also central here. Online, regular navigation routines can involve all manner of harmful content, exposure to which may be a function of intent completely beyond the victim's choices due to the high degree of overlap between the social spaces of both targets and offenders in that setting. A user may be navigating in any number of content-driven or networking-driven platforms and be exposed to negative content from numerous sources. Though victimisation offline can also be experienced in places considered safe, that online navigational sphere considered free from risk may be more difficult to gauge due to the hidden nature of content creators until harmful material is actually experienced.

The frameworks of LET and RAT provide valuable insight into risk factors that can be built upon with phenomena common in the online setting today. First, the number of motivated offenders potentially able to reach a victim should be taken into account, in addition to the lowered cost of aggression afforded by ease of communication. As such, in terms of LET, the distribution of risk, or likelihood of victimisation, is affected by both increased numbers of aggressors and access that is relatively independent of the online behaviours of victims. Furthermore, the potential negative effects of lessened social presence in lowering accountability should be included, in addition to the remarkably broad reach of aggressor material meant to hurt when disseminated online. In terms of new issues central to RAT, these tools available in the online environment create convergence of risk components on a massive scale. However, offenders, targets and level of guardianship need not converge in shared physical space or even at the same time. The hateful intent of the aggressor can reach the target, causing potentially harmful effects, even without the knowledge of the originator but based on the capabilities for access and dissemination unique to the Internet.

The visibility of the suitable target should also be acknowledged, given the global scale of personal visibility, for example through social media. Again, specific targeting is not required to create a significant risk online. Hate material can be created and spread globally without aggressor knowledge of who will be victimised by it. Here, hate material can carry second- and third-degree effects much sooner and to a wider audience than would be possible offline. Third, effective guardianship in the online setting is difficult when material and threats can arrive by so many avenues, whether through text, video, image or otherwise. Keeping these problems in mind, after a more thorough assessment of online hate as it exists today, we propose a novel theoretical model in Chapter 5 that combines social identity dynamics, unique online environmental risk factors and the risk of online hate.

A new theoretical approach that takes into consideration the unique characteristics of the online setting in terms of visibility, accessibility and aggressor capability, combined with the issues of anonymity and content dissemination, would help to fill the gaps inherent in the primarily offline theoretical frameworks of LET and RAT. This new perspective should use these key interactional phenomena to assess the likelihood of victimisation, in addition to delving into the structural issues inherent in the online environment that may reinforce certain negative behaviours. Indeed, this would encompass three areas, namely the perspective of the victim and the aggressor through situational interactions, the capabilities of aggressors to create content, and personal characteristics that may be reinforced by the mechanisms built into the online setting.

While discussing our general theoretical approach, we also wish to acknowledge the surrounding societal context. One important aspect missing from preceding research on exposure to online hate is that of cross-cultural differences. In particular, a vast majority of empirical studies concerning negative aspects of Internet usage such as online hate or online risk focus on samples from single countries. This means that the findings might be restricted to only one context, thus limiting knowledge on what they could mean in a wider global perspective. A lack of comparative data also prohibits plausible theoretical discussions based on empirical findings, for instance in making evaluations regarding the proportion of users who become exposed to hateful or harmful online contents.

Throughout this book, we argue that theoretical notions are valid and useful only when they are applied in the right context. Our theoretical foundations are applicable relatively universally. In other words, the propositions of LET and RAT can be applied to various situations associated with online activities and exposure to hate. Our empirical data come from societies in which computers, mobile phones and social media platforms are unavoidable tools in the everyday lives of all young people. Despite this, even the behavioural patterns of Internet use differ considerably among the four countries examined. Therefore, while looking at exposure to hate at the individual level, we also need to acknowledge certain institutional characteristics that differentiate these countries. We will discuss these characteristics from both cultural and legal perspectives, which together help us to position the empirical observations as to why the rates of online exposure to hate are different across the countries under study.

References

Choi, K. (2008). Computer crime victimisation and integrated theory: An empirical assessment. *International Journal of Cyber Criminology, 2*(1), 308–333. Retrieved from www.cybercrimejournal.com/Choiijccjan2008.htm.

Cohen, L. E. (1981). Modeling crime trends: A criminal opportunity perspective. *Journal of Research in Crime and Delinquency, 18*(1), 138–164. DOI: 10.2307/2094935.

Cohen, L. E., & Felson, M. (1979). Social change and crime rate trends: A routine activity approach. *American Sociological Review, 44*(4), 588–608. DOI: 10.2307/2094589.

Cohen, L. E., Kluegel, J. R., & Land, K. C. (1981). Social inequality and predatory criminal victimization: An exposition and test of a formal theory. *American Sociological Review, 46*(5), 505–524. DOI: 10.2307/2094935.

Felson, M., & Boba, R. (2010). *Crime and Everyday Life*. London: Sage. DOI: 10.4135/9781483349299.

Hindelang, M., Gottfredson, M., & Garofalo, J. (1978). *Victims of Personal Crime: An Empirical Foundation for a Theory of Personal Victimization*. Cambridge, MA: Ballinger. DOI: 10.2307/2066613.

Holt, T. J., & Bossler, A. M. (2008). Examining the applicability of lifestyle-routine activities theory for cybercrime victimisation. *Deviant Behavior, 30*(1), 1–25. DOI: 10.1080/01639620701876577.

Holt, T. J., Bossler, A. M., Malinski, R., & May, D. C. (2016). Identifying predictors of unwanted online sexual conversations among youth using a low self-control and routine activity framework. *Journal of Contemporary Criminal Justice, 32*(2), 108–128. DOI: 10.1177/1043986215621376.

Holt, T. J., Fitzgerald, S., Bossler, A. M., Chee, G., & Ng, E. (2015). Assessing the risk factors of cyber and mobile phone bullying victimization in a nationally representative sample of Singapore youth. *International Journal of Offender Therapy and Comparative Criminology* (advance online publication). DOI: 10.1177/0306624X14554852.

Keipi, T., & Oksanen, A. (2014). Self-exploration, anonymity and risks in the online setting: analysis of narratives by 14–18-year olds. *Journal of Youth Studies, 17*, 1097–1113. DOI: 10.1080/13676261.2014.881988.

Kigerl, A. (2011). Routine activity theory and the determinants of high cybercrime countries. *Social Science Computer Review*, 0894439311422689. DOI: 10.1177/0894439 311422689.

Leukfeldt, E. R. (2014). Phishing for suitable targets in the Netherlands: Routine activity theory and phishing victimization. *Cyberpsychology, Behavior, and Social Networking*, *17*(8), 551–555. DOI: 10.1089/cyber.2014.0008.

Leukfeldt, E. R., & Yar, M. (2016). Applying routine activity theory to cybercrime: A theoretical and empirical analysis. *Deviant Behavior*, *37*(3), 1–18. DOI: 10.1080/ 01639625.2015.1012409.

Marcum, C. D., Higgins, G. E., & Ricketts, M. L. (2010). Potential factors of online victimization of youth: An examination of adolescent online behaviors utilizing routine activity theory. *Deviant Behavior*, *31*(5), 381–410. DOI: 10.1080/01639620903004903.

Meier, R. F., & Miethe, T. D. (1993). Understanding theories of criminal victimization. *Crime and Justice*, *17*, 459–499. Retrieved from www.jstor.org/stable/1147556.

Mitchell, K. J., Finkelhor, D., Jones, L. M., & Wolak, J. (2010). Use of social networking sites in online sex crimes against minors: An examination of national incidence and means of utilization. *Journal of Adolescent Health*, *47*(2), 183–190. DOI: 10.1016/j. jadohealth.2010.01.007.

Mitchell, K. J., Jones, L. M., Finkelhor, D., & Wolak, J. (2013). Understanding the decline in unwanted online sexual solicitations for US youth 2000–2010: Findings from three Youth Internet Safety Surveys. *Child Abuse & Neglect*, *37*(12), 1225–1236. DOI: 10.1016/j.chiabu.2013.07.002.

Näsi, M., Oksanen, A., Keipi, T., & Räsänen, P. (2015). Cybercrime victimization among young people: A multi-nation study. *Journal of Scandinavian Studies in Criminology and Crime Prevention*, *16*(2), 203–210. DOI: 10.1080/14043858.2015. 1046640.

Pratt, T. C., & Turanovic, J. J. (2016). Lifestyle and routine activity theories revisited: The importance of "risk" to the study of victimization. *Victims & Offenders*, *11*(3), 335–354. DOI: 10.1080/15564886.2015.1057351.

Pratt, T. C., Holtfreter, K., & Reisig, M. D. (2010). Routine online activity and Internet fraud targeting: Extending the generality of routine activity theory. *Journal of Research in Crime and Delinquency*, *47*(3), 267–296. DOI: 10.1177/0022427810365903.

Reyns, B. W. (2013). Online routines and identity theft victimisation further expanding routine activity theory beyond direct-contact offenses. *Journal of Research in Crime and Delinquency*, *50*(2), 216–238.DOI: 10.1177/0022427811425539.

Reyns, B. W., Henson, B., & Fisher, B. S. (2011). Being pursued online applying cyberlifestyle–routine activities theory to cyberstalking victimisation. *Criminal Justice and Behaviour*, *38*(11), 1149–1169. DOI: 10.1177/0093854811421448.

Reyns, B. W., Henson, B., & Fisher, B. S. (2015). Guardians of the cyber galaxy An empirical and theoretical analysis of the guardianship concept from routine activity theory as it applies to online forms of victimization. *Journal of Contemporary Criminal Justice,* *32*(2), 148–168. DOI: 1043986215621378.

Stewart, E. A., Elifson, K. W., & Sterk, C. E. (2004). Integrating the general theory of crime into an explanation of violent victimization among female offenders. *Justice Quarterly*, *21*(1), 159–181. DOI: 10.1080/07418820400095771.

Tewksbury, R., & Mustaine, E. E. (2000). Routine activities and vandalism: A theoretical and empirical study. *Journal of Crime and Justice*, *23*(1), 81–110. DOI: 10.1080/ 0735648X.2000.9721111.

van Wilsem, J. (2013). Hacking and harassment – Do they have something in common? Comparing risk factors for online victimization. *Journal of Contemporary Criminal Justice, 29*(4), 437–453. DOI: 10.1177/1043986213507402.

Wilcox, P., Sullivan, C. J., Jones, S., & Van Gelder, J. (2014). Personality and opportunity: An integrated approach to offending and victimization. *Criminal Justice and Behavior, 41*, 880–901. DOI: 10.1177/0093854813520603.

Yar, M. (2005). The novelty of "cybercrime": An assessment in light of routine activity theory. *European Journal of Criminology, 2*(4), 407–427. DOI: 10.1177/14773708 0556056.

4   The rise of online hate

4.1 From bigotry to hate crime

On 15 May 2010 a man posted a message on a social media discussion board
stating his plans to shoot the Finnish Prime Minister and Minister of Finance,
after which he would set off a bomb in the house of parliament. The man was
reported to the police and was subsequently charged with threatening behaviour.
However, the Supreme Court of Finland later found the suspect not guilty
(HelHO:2012:1). The verdict was due partly to a loophole in the law which
states that the potential victims must be aware of the threat and feel threatened
by it. It is this intersection between the law and the right to express plans,
thoughts or opinions in the online context that prompts us to take a closer look at
the landscape in which we currently live.

The growing role of the Internet in the wider societal context has been rapid,
to the extent of having developed faster than laws intended to protect its users.
Now, aggravated and hateful behaviour have always played some part in human
interaction, but it is the emergence of the Internet and different social media that
have helped to push many aspects of negative and anti-social behaviour into the
wider public forum. A few decades ago, the aforementioned disgruntled Finnish
man would likely have merely expressed his thoughts in the corner of a local
pub to a small audience. However, the tools available to us today allow such
messages to be amplified through various avenues of social media to reach a far
wider audience.

Hate aimed at individuals or specific groups of people is actualised in both
speech and action. It is grounded on ideology and prejudice that are modified
culturally and reinforced in everyday interaction. Although bigotry has been a
familiar concept throughout history, the idea of hate content as a crime is new
(Gerstenfeld, 2013, p. 2). Hate crime typically refers to targeted crime motivated by prejudice, for example on the part of certain social groups linked by
racist views. In the online context, hate becomes criminal only if there are laws
classifying behaviour in terms of what can and cannot be said. The approaches
taken in this classification differ cross-nationally. For instance, the United
States has adopted a more liberal stance on what content is allowed, largely on
the basis of the First Amendment and freedom of speech. On the other hand,

many European societies have enacted laws which regulate statements that threaten or insult a specific group of people (Hawdon, Oksanen & Räsänen, 2016; Waldron, 2012). These laws vary from country to country, however, and so do the sanctions for breaking them. The need to balance freedom of expression with safeguards, especially given the expansion of online communication, has induced many European nations to establish better ways of regulating online hate speech.

Although the terms "hate crime" and "hate speech" are in common use, various scholars emphasise that defining hate is actually a highly complex task, and that it is very difficult to distinguish what is hate speech from what is not (Citron & Norton, 2011; Foxman & Wolf, 2013; Waldron, 2012). The reason for this lies in the often unclear dichotomy between the rational or ideological side of hate and the irrational and highly emotional side, as they can both coexist to varying degrees. Defining hate becomes far simpler in the case of extreme actions carried out by individuals or groups. Extreme acts such as mass murders or terrorist attacks are manifestations of hate and do not require debate as to whether or not hate was involved. However, at the other end of the hate classification spectrum, the right to express hate clashes with calls for limits on the free expression of opinion. Definitions are also liable to be manipulated. Some of the most notorious hate groups have been clever enough to exploit these disagreements. For example, the Ku Klux Klan (KKK) claims to represent love of its own race rather than targeted hate of another.

The Council of Europe has sought to raise awareness of online hate speech with the *Young People Combating Hate Speech Online* campaign (2012–2014). According to the Council, hate speech

> covers all forms of expression which spread, incite, promote or justify racial hatred, xenophobia, anti-Semitism or other forms of hatred based on intolerance, including: intolerance expressed by aggressive nationalism and ethnocentrism, discrimination and hostility against minorities, migrants and people of immigrant origin.
>
> (Council of Europe, 2013; see also Banks, 2011)

This formulation includes many, but not all, potential forms of hate.

In 2016, the European Commission against Racism and Intolerance (ECRI) released a general policy recommendation on combating the expression of hate in any medium from the written or spoken word to cultural products such as paintings, music or videos. Their sixty-six-page report includes guidelines on how to prevent the expression of hate and how to counter it. It recommends that EU states should sanction hate speech while also safeguarding freedom of expression. This represents a challenging balance. Besides legal sanctions and regulations, ECRI underlines self-regulation and the importance of raising awareness. Their definition of hate speech is wide and aims to cover its most distinctive forms:

Hate speech … entails the use of one or more particular forms of expression – namely, the advocacy, promotion or incitement of the denigration, hatred or vilification of a person or group of persons, as well any harassment, insult, negative stereotyping, stigmatisation or threat of such person or persons and any justification of all these forms of expression – that is based on a non-exhaustive list of personal characteristics or status that includes "race", colour, language, religion or belief, nationality or national or ethnic origin, as well as descent, age, disability, sex, gender, gender identity and sexual orientation.

(ECRI, 2016, p. 16)

Our perspective is that hate and aggression are potentially everywhere in human interaction, and that they are not necessarily limited to the most well-known examples such as racism and religious bigotry. The potential for hatred includes harmful and threatening statements involving the active targeting of individuals or larger human collectives. We begin our review with organised hate groups that may act violently or simply concentrate on the dissemination of hate propaganda. Notably, the most common forms of online hatred are not necessarily expressed by these notorious groups but rather by ordinary, less visibly affiliated individuals. As such, we will show how hate has become a part of everyday reality online through various forms.

Keeping in mind the complexity of defining hate content (e.g. Blazak, 2009; Citron, 2014; Douglas, 2007; Wall, 2001), we build on the work of Franklin (2002) by defining online hate expression as the use of information and communications technology (ICT) to "advocate violence against, separation from, defamation of, deception about or hostility towards others" (p. 2). We therefore focus on individuals or groups who use ICT to express sentiments that attack others based on race, national origin, gender, ethnicity, sexual orientation, religion, or any other characteristic that defines a particular group.

It is important to note that exposure to online hate creates a distinct form of victimisation, as abuse is purposely targeted at a collective identity. Given the multifaceted nature of the Internet, involving all manner of expressional and interactional tools, we consider any form of expression that targets the identity of a group of individuals to be hate speech and hate material (Hawdon, Oksanen & Räsänen, 2014; Oksanen, Hawdon, Holker, Näsi & Räsänen, 2014). Consequently we use the classifications of hate speech or hate material interchangeably and also consider any material fitting the above description as relevant to the purposes of this book. It is also important to note that in our approach, and in the data involved in the studies included, the context of harmful online content is also founded on respondents' own-perception of material that they themselves found hateful or degrading and that inappropriately attacked certain collectives or individuals.

4.2 Organised hate groups

Hate is disseminated by both individuals and organised hate groups. Hate groups may have a wide variety of targets and ideological views, ranging from terrorist organisations to gangs of various types, often not identifying themselves as hate groups (Gerstenfeld, 2013, pp. 130–131; Oksanen, Räsänen & Hawdon, 2014). Though they are varied, these groups share the common denominators of comprising a number of individuals, being organised to some extent, and publicly targeting either private individuals or groups. As such, they only exist when there is something to oppose. Hate groups are also based on very stark distinctions between an ingroup (*us*) and an outgroup (*them*). This very basic distinction may, in certain social conditions, increase prejudice against others, as noted in social psychology (Brown, 2010; Tajfel, 1970). In specific social and historic conditions, outgroup members are devalued or even dehumanised. In such conditions, ingroup attachment to violent ideologies can facilitate violence.

The US has, in many respects, constituted a safe haven for organised hate groups, including well-known examples such as the KKK, Holocaust Denial and Christian Identity. The KKK has famously influenced US politics in many different eras, with the US history of fighting hate having often been relatively unsuccessful. For example, the Southern Poverty Law Center monitors the actions of over 1,600 US extremist and hate groups. These include a wide range from anti-immigrant groups, white nationalists and black separatists to various extreme Christian hate groups. Furthermore, added to this list are organised or semi-organised terrorist organisations (e.g. Blazak, 2009). For example, it is difficult to consider ISIS anything other than a terrorist hate group.

Hate groups have always been skilled users of mass media and technological innovations. Technological developments over the past thirty years have facilitated and improved the effectiveness of their tasks remarkably. White supremacists in the US were among the very early users of the electronic communication network during the 1980s. Hate is said to have gone online as early as March 1984 when neo-Nazi publisher George Dietz used the bulletin board system (BBS) as a method of online communication. The White Aryan Resistance BBS followed, adopting this form of communication in 1984 and 1985 (Berlet, 2001). At that time linking two computers via BBS was very unusual, as it was only commercialised in the 1980s with faster modems. These first developments are, however, a good reminder that online hate and aggression are not new phenomena.

The first online hate site appeared soon after the introduction of the World Wide Web. Stormfront.org, thought to be the first major hate site, started in 1995 (Bowman-Grieve, 2009; Brown, 2009). Although some other minor hate sites had been created at this time, Stormfront.org was initiated by Grand Wizard of the KKK Don Black, who was able to take this new format to a new level in terms of both depth and content (Levin, 2002). Stormfront.org gradually became more popular and expanded rapidly, continuing into the 2000s. By 2009, the site had over 159,000 members (Bowman-Grieve, 2009) and by 2015 the number of registered users of Stormfront.org was approximately 300,000 (Potok, 2016). Although its user numbers have continued to rise, as of 2015 Stormfront had a rank of only 13,648 on the list of the most popular sites online (Potok, 2015).

It was during the 1990s that organised hate groups became increasingly active online. During that time there were, on average, 400 hate sites and dozens of KKK, neo-Nazi, racist skinhead, Christian Identity and black separatist organisations sites as well. Besides websites such as Stormfront.org, different discussion forums became the main channels for spreading hate-filled ideologies during the 1990s and early 2000s. With the rise of social media during the 2000s, involving the development of various social platforms fostering personal expression, feedback and interaction, the Internet gradually became more interactive. This development has certainly changed the overall picture of online hate. Social media have made online hate communication more viral and visible than ever before. As Foxman and Wolf (2013, p. 11) state, the rise of social media has been a game changer:

> A few years back, we might have dismissed the anti-Semitic groups, racist organisations, and other vicious haters on the Internet as outliers … not worth taking seriously or responding to. But today we live in the world of Web 2.0, which has transformed the way the Internet is being used. In the interactive community environment of Web 2.0, social networking connects hundreds of millions of people around the globe; it takes just one "friend of a friend" to infect a circle of hundreds or thousands of individuals with weird, hateful lies that may go unchallenged, twisting minds in unpredictable ways. And with the users of Web 2.0 comprised largely of younger people, the impact of the misinformation contained there may persist for generations to come.

Social media have allowed hate groups to be increasingly visible and successful in reaching and recruiting significant numbers of Internet users. Hate groups have been known to actively recruit young people using online technology (Lee & Leets, 2002). Young people are considered the age group most vulnerable to these recruiting methods. The existence of these groups has become a permanent online phenomenon (Chau & Xu, 2007). According to the Southern Poverty Law Center that regularly monitors online hate and radical groups, the number of active US hate groups fell after peaking in 2011. At the end of 2015, there were 892 active hate groups online. It is believed that activism has shifted towards lone wolves such as Dylann Roof, who murdered nine African Americans in a church shooting in the summer of 2015 (Potok, 2016).

Hate groups are by no means diminishing, despite this small decline in the US after the peak in 2011, as between 2014 and 2015 the number of hate groups witnessed a 14 per cent increase (Potok, 2016). Current Internet platforms provide better access than ever before for any and all activists wishing to find like-minded peers online. The Internet and later social media have facilitated the rise of an international extremist community (Burris, Smith & Strahm, 2000;

2014-15 ~ a 14% increase

Gerstenfeld, 2013). These groups and their members are active in sharing and disseminating information that potentially encourages lone wolves who are motivated towards radical actions and actively seek a community to validate those motivations. Norwegian terrorist Anders Behring Breivik, school shooters and young ISIS recruits are just a few examples of people who have been motivated and validated by hate online.

4.3 Everyday hate and social media

Hate projects powerful images. In considering hate, the white robes of the Ku Klux Klan, swastikas or skinheads may come to mind. However, it is a common mistake to consider hate mongers as total loners or members of an organised hate group which is working to destroy the very cornerstones of civilised societies. Those individuals emailing hateful messages are not necessarily total outsiders separated from the everyday life of most people, as they are likely to belong to the same social circles and age groups as many of the victims. The creators of harmful content may be classmates, neighbours, or members of the same clubs or hobby groups as their victims, and have social contact with them outside the online setting. Gerstenfeld (2013, p. 5) reminds us of this misconception in her book on hate crimes:

> It is tempting for many of us to feel smugly superior to those who perpetrate hate crimes and to think of them as deviants and fanatics. ... [H]owever, most hate crime offenders do not fit this profile. In fact, for the most part, they are us.

Various types of hateful content were available for broader audiences long before the introduction of the Internet. Before the Internet, there was radio and television; before that, print media. Different tools of communication have provided avenues for sending, receiving and retrieving disturbing and criminal material, for example books and newsletters. Both the KKK in the US and the National Socialist Party in Germany during the early twentieth century shared the characteristic of successfully using the newest available technology, namely radio and film (Levin, 2002). Both groups used existing prejudices and available technologies, and exploited economic and social crises to leverage power for themselves.

Since the Internet, and social media in particular, became the most important communication tool in everyday life, the capacity for spreading all types of content, including hate, has increased. First of all, similar opportunities are provided to virtually any user who has access to the Internet, while in the past significant resources and connections were needed to effectively have a message widely distributed for consumption. Second, any of these users has access to this global stage while also having the ability to customise how they are perceived in terms of both identifiability and visibility. In online interaction and expression, users can hide behind a form of anonymity through a username or a created profile that has been customised to meet personal needs. Third, social media and ICTs create fast-paced communication environments where physical cues and traditional feedback become less important.

Already over thirty years ago, studies showed the prevalence of uninhibited behaviour and angry messages in anonymous computer-mediated communication, a phenomenon already termed then as "flaming" (Kiesler, Siegel & McGuire, 1984). Anonymity is naturally one factor behind this behaviour, but it does not directly cause aggression or negative sentiment. Rather, anonymity is a tool that can diminish the costs of expression, even if negative, due to relative freedom from external pressures linked to social norms, feedback and accountability. This interactive aggression through technological devices is thus something that has been known for some time as a significant phenomenon in technologically mediated communication. The negative sides of anonymity can still be witnessed in platforms giving users the tools to express themselves freely without direct incentive-altering consequences.

What is perhaps most striking is that users do not necessarily hide their identities when targeting others with negative content. Users have now become accustomed to saying things publicly via their Facebook profiles, including extreme viewpoints advocating harm to others. In Finland, for example, the Minister of Migration and European Affairs Astrid Thors filed a report to police for the investigation of a Facebook group named, "I'm prepared to do some jail time for killing Astrid Thors!" Similar incidents have also recently taken place in other countries as well. Politicians and celebrities are often the targets of online aggression, due to their stances on certain issues or simply lifestyle choices. These very heated conversations do not necessarily concern societal topics such as immigration or politics at large; even personal decisions such as diet and health habits can be chosen as points of severe contention (Pöyhtäri, Haara & Raittila, 2013).

As mentioned, almost anything can cause people to become upset online, and almost anything can eventually lead to hateful communication. Much of the hateful communication, regardless of focus, is disseminated within the everyday online settings where people spend much of their interactional and expressional time. Notably, online hate overlaps with both cyberbullying and online harassment, which by definition involve threats or other offensive behaviour targeted at individuals (see Jones, Mitchell & Finkelhor, 2013). Online hate is also linked to cybercrime, including some forms of online harassment, stalking and defamation. Hate content can also blend in with other types of everyday aggression. Hence, we should pay attention not only to the most radical organised hate groups or lone wolves, but also to the ways in which rhetoric is openly used in social media consumed on a wider scale where users may not be expecting such aggression.

Now in the second decade of the new millennium, the Internet and social media have become saturated with content that informs and inspires both young and old. Approximately 90 per cent of working-aged individuals in Europe and North America are active users (World Internet Statistics, 2016). The online setting provides convenient tools with which users may fulfil both personal and group motivations, whether beneficial or destructive. By providing instantaneous access without a system of identification, the Internet permits groups and individuals espousing hate to transmit their ideas to a worldwide audience. The stage of expression has become global and generally accessible to all users equally. This holds implications in terms of the scope of potential damage through increased audience, effectiveness of targeting and heightened hate motivation through knowledge of wide-scale content visibility.

These interpretations are not equally valid across all countries. The rates of both victimisation and exposure to online hate may vary as well. This has been established in earlier research through several extensive cross-national comparisons on school bullying (e.g. Currie et al., 2008; Elgar et al., 2015). Craig and colleagues (2009), for instance, provide a comprehensive study on bullying and victimisation among children and teenagers using representative survey data collected at schools from forty nations. According to their findings, exposure to bullying varied from less than 10 per cent to over 45 per cent for boys, and less than 5 per cent to over 35 per cent for girls. They examined direct and indirect forms of bullying, both physical and verbal. Adolescents in northern Europe reported less bullying and victimisation than those in Eastern Europe, Central Europe and the American continent.

Similar interpretations of the online world can be made, although there is not, as yet, an abundance of research on cyberbullying globally. In the European context, however, rates of younger people who have been bullied online tend to vary. One of the most noteworthy findings of the 2010 EU Kids Online survey was that approximately 6 per cent of 9–16-year-old children reported that they had been bullied. However, in Estonia and Romania, the percentages were much higher, at 14 and 13 per cent respectively. In Italy, on the other hand, the proportion of bullied children was very low at just 2 per cent (Livingstone, Haddon, Görzig & Ólafsson, 2011). In addition, different studies conducted on cybercrime victimisation show differences between countries (e.g. Näsi, Oksanen, Keipi & Räsänen, 2015; Reyns, Henson & Fisher, 2011).

In general, the findings from preceding comparative studies give an important insight. Even in the online world, geographical locations and national borders do make a difference. Therefore, we should also seek to examine how all of the differences between the countries studied translate into the online context, despite the increasing overlap between online and offline interaction and many of the everyday activities that are carried out in both. The Internet and social media have become saturated with content that informs and inspires both young and old individuals. However, by providing instantaneous access without a system to easily identify interacting participants, the Internet permits groups and individuals espousing hate to transmit their ideas to a worldwide audience at a higher impact than has been possible before.

4.4 Exposure to online hate from a cross-national perspective

Based on recent comparative survey data, we are able to give an empirical overview of online hate. The data are drawn from a cross-sectional survey carried out in 2013 and 2014, targeted at teenagers and young adults aged between 15 and 30. The questions addressed young people's online activities, social activities, subjective wellbeing, self-esteem and trust as well online hate. We did not market our survey as a "hate speech" survey and questions concerning online hate were placed in the middle of the survey, as explained below.

Data description

> The empirical examples presented in this book come from unique cross-sectional surveys, conducted in four nations. The data were collected as part of the research project "Hate Communities: A Cross-national Comparison" (funded by the Kone Foundation, 2012–2016). The project's YouNet2013 and YouNet2014 surveys included socio-demographic variables and questions about online activity, online risks and online hate content. We also enquired into online and offline interactions, social trust, self-esteem, life satisfaction and violent victimisation. Respondents were given a chance to provide feedback to the research team concerning the survey. The research team originally designed the surveys in English, with native Finnish and German speakers translating the survey into Finnish and German respectively. The questionnaires were then back-translated into English and compared with the original surveys. The surveys were pre-tested with students at the University of Turku, Finland, and at Virginia Tech in the US.
>
> The data for Finland ($n=555$) and the US ($n=1,033$) were collected in the spring of 2013 while the data for Germany ($n=978$) and the UK ($n=999$) were collected in the spring of 2014. Respondents to each survey were recruited from a demographically balanced panel and the respondents voluntarily agreed to participate in research surveys (for details, see Näsi et al., 2014). The quota sample sizes were estimated by Survey Sampling International (SSI), a company which was also responsible for the recruitment of the survey respondents. SSI is a global provider of data solutions and technology for consumer and business-to-business survey research (SSI, 2016).

The most common method for estimating the prevalence of hate and harmful content in everyday life is to measure subjective experiences of exposure. In order to measure exposure to online hate, the respondents in our study were asked, "In the past three months, have you seen hateful or degrading writings or speech online, which inappropriately attacked certain groups of people or individuals?" Figure 4.1 shows the proportions of 15–30-year-olds who had witnessed online hate (i.e. cyberhate) in each dataset.

The average rate of exposure in the four countries was approximately 42 per cent. But as Figure 4.1 shows, the proportion of respondents who were exposed

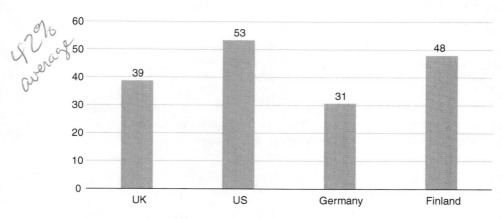

Figure 4.1 Exposure to online hate among 15–30-year-old respondents in the UK, the US, Germany and Finland. Percentages.

to online hate materials varies by country. Approximately 53 per cent of American, 48 per cent of Finnish and 39 per cent of British respondents reported having been exposed to online hate material. The differences are very significant in statistical terms ($p<0.001$). The proportion is somewhat lower in Germany, with 31 per cent having been exposed. In this sense, we can say that of the surveyed adolescents and young adults, a notable share had witnessed hateful or degrading material.

Compared to the high figures for exposure to online hate, very few of our survey respondents admitted to producing online material that other people interpreted as hateful or degrading. In percentages, these figures are 4.1 for the US, 4.0 for Finland, 3.4 for the UK and 0.9 for Germany (Kaakinen et al., 2016). Even fewer admitted to being a member of a group that produces online material that other people interpret as hateful or degrading (in the US 2.4 per cent, Finland 2.2 per cent, UK 1.1 per cent, and 0.4 per cent in Germany). These proportions are quite understandable given the global audience and potentially significant effects that a few content creators can have on many online consumers. Hence, the relatively high rates of exposure to online hate in different countries should not lead to the assumption of there being an equivalence in content producers. Nevertheless, we have a wide range of potential actors contributing to the phenomenon, ranging from single actors to various online groups, more than enough to negatively affect the lives of a significant portion of Internet users.

When discussing the rates of exposure, it is also important to evaluate how the users find hate materials in the first place. Our survey included a question concerning how the respondents happened to see online hate material. Naturally, this item was shown only to those respondents who reported that they had come across the sites showing hateful or degrading material. The questionnaire had three options to choose from. First, "I deliberately found my way"; second,

"I got the link to the site from a friend or acquaintance of mine"; and third, "I got there by accident". Figure 4.2 shows the responses by country.

The general pattern of responses is relatively clear in all countries, although differences also exist between them. The general pattern is that most of the respondents were not actively seeking hate material. This is perhaps not surprising, since in most discussions both researchers and practitioners tend to worry primarily about young people who become exposed to violence, pornography and other potentially harmful material through the choices of others (e.g. Foxman & Wolf, 2013; Livingstone et al., 2011). In Finland and Germany, 66 per cent of the 15–30-year-old respondents reported that they ended up on the hate sites accidently. In the UK and the US the responses were lower (with 50 and 42 per cent), but still clearly higher than other categories. Figure 4.2 also shows that the impact of social contacts is very important online. In the UK, the US and Germany, approximately one-fifth of the respondents received a link from their friends or acquaintances that led to sites showing hate material. In Finland, only 11 per cent reported having received a link which directed them to those sites. However, what is also noteworthy is that many users saw hate material as a result of deliberate action. This means that they either sought out hateful content or were interested in familiarising themselves with such material. Cross-country differences are considerable here as well. In the US, 37 per cent of the respondents said they ended up on sites showing hate material deliberately. The numbers are lower for other countries (29 per cent in the UK, 23 per cent in Finland, and 16 per cent in Germany).

Figure 4.2 gives us insight into the ways in which teenagers and young adults end up seeing hateful material online. Most reached hate sites by accident, with deliberate visits being far less common. This is an important reminder of the potential threats that new communication technologies pose for average online

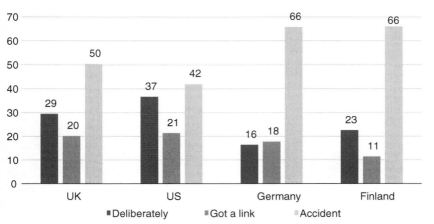

Figure 4.2 How respondents happened to find online hate content in the UK, US, Germany and Finland. Percentages for those exposed to online hate.

users. Similarly, another important question has to do with which services and media platforms were associated with exposure to hate material. It is well known that young people are especially active in certain social media platforms, such as Facebook, Instagram and Twitter. On the other hand, it is possible that certain types of hate material are available in less used services, such as personal homepages or message boards. Notably, proponents of hate are increasingly bridging the gaps between concrete violence and online material. For example, ISIS has been recruiting young people who are highly active on various forms of social media through these very channels. Propaganda involving the motivation of hate is made easily discoverable online as a first step in strategic action by dangerous groups to attract young people who may share their views to some extent, in order to encourage further harmful behaviour.

At the general level, we do not know which of the different online services should be regarded as potentially dangerous across the four countries, but our data do give information on this issue. The questionnaire included a question regarding different online services where hateful or degrading material was seen. Again, this question was shown only to those who reported having been exposed to online hate material. The respondents were given a list of the thirteen most common online services (ranging from social media to photo-sharing sites and online games) and were asked to assess each. Table 4.1 lists different platforms and services in which the respondents said they saw hate material.

As the table shows, the most popular online services are also the most common sources of hate material. Facebook was clearly the most common site for witnessing hate material in all the countries. YouTube appeared to be the second most common source of exposure, although it was clearly behind Facebook in all four countries. At the same time, the prevalence of hate material seen in different online sites tended to vary from country to country. For example, notable differences by country were observed when comparing Twitter and

Table 4.1 Exposure to hate in SNS sites and online environments in the UK, the US, Germany and Finland. Percentages for those exposed to online hate

	UK	US	Germany	Finland
Facebook	63.8	62.8	77.3	48.1
YouTube	37.0	47.9	43.5	37.2
Twitter	26.1	21.1	8.7	3.8
Tumblr	12.9	14.2	4.0	3.0
Wikipedia	4.9	4.5	3.7	1.9
General message board	15.2	19.2	14.7	41.4
Newspaper message boards	7.0	6.4	14.0	21.8
Blogs	8.3	13.2	7.7	16.2
Home pages	2.3	5.4	6.4	5.3
Photosharing sites (e.g. Instagram)	4.1	6.5	2.7	3.8
Online games	4.4	6.4	4.7	4.9
Instant messengers	4.1	4.2	3.7	1.5
Pop-up sites	4.7	5.6	2.0	1.5

general message boards. Over 20 per cent of those exposed to online hate in the UK and the US saw such material on Twitter. The number was only 8 per cent in Germany, and only 4 per cent in Finland. Despite this, more than 40 per cent of Finnish respondents who were exposed to hate content witnessed such material on general discussion boards. The proportions were less than 20 per cent in all other countries.

Together, the findings above reflect the fact that young online users in different countries tend to be active in different online media. In addition, various sites are likely used for varying purposes in different countries. As already discussed in Chapter 1, several interpretations have been given as to why cross-national variations in exposure rates exist. On the one hand, the clear difference between the UK and the US is interesting. Both of these countries are English-speaking and share many cultural characteristics. On the other hand, it is somewhat surprising that the exposure rate in Finland comes close to that of the US. Finland is often considered a Nordic welfare state, a homogenous country characterised by a low level of social and economic inequality between population groups. One of the key features of Finland contributing to this low economic inequality is a far-reaching welfare network allowing for effective redistribution of wealth in society. The US is typically referred to as a more capitalist country, which generally enforces individual freedom and price competition within various markets (e.g. Kvist, Fritzell, Hvinden & Kangas, 2012; Mishra, 2014). Yet, despite these institutional differences in income inequality and heterogeneity of population that in the past have been linked to social instability, the hate exposure figures of these two countries deviate only slightly.

One possible interpretation of the cross-country variation relates to the role of society type in terms of ICT infrastructure and overall Internet use patterns. All four nations are among the world's leaders for Internet user penetration rates. According to recent statistics (Internet Live Stats, 2014), the Internet penetration rate was 87 per cent in the US and 94 per cent in Finland. The rates were lower in the UK and Germany, of 89 and 87 per cent, than in Finland. Since the Internet is used more frequently in Finland than in the UK or Germany, these and other types of individual-level factors can result in national differences. Furthermore, in addition to Internet use rates, there is the issue of how users interpret online content. It is possible that users from different countries relate to harmful content differently, classifying certain content as benign that users from other nations might take as negative. In this case, Finnish and US responses to online hate were similar, pointing to a convergence of online reaction independent of cultural borders.

In preceding research, cross-national differences in ICT use have been summarised in terms of cultural or legal characteristics that separate countries from each other (e.g. Barbosa & Faria, 2011; Räsänen, 2006). Broadly speaking, cultural differences between societies mean that there are political, economic and/or social differences between them that can be understood in the light of certain cultural features. These differences can refer to specific arrangements that create varying structural conditions for citizens to engage in particular activities.

The distinctive structural characteristics of a country result from various historical and political processes within it. Welfare state classifications involve the idea that state variation and development can be described through a typology of different societal characteristics (e.g. Arts & Gelissen, 2002; Esping-Andersen, 1993). Similarities and differences between welfare state types have been found to have significant effects on many dimensions of individual life conditions, social activities and cultural participation (Kvist et al., 2012; Räsänen, 2006). Here, it can be assumed that political and social institutions also influence exposure to hate material online, via the extent to which online activities are structurally determined by different socio-demographic factors and cultural customs. For instance, the UK, the US and Finland are often characterised as being different in terms of ethnicity, political climate, trade union participation or gender equality. These general differences thus provide the potential for formulating a feasible method of understanding the effects on Internet connectivity and exposure to online hate in different countries.

Along with specific cultural features, however, we also need to acknowledge the differences in jurisdiction between the four countries. All of these nations have constitutional guarantees of free speech, yet they vary in the extent to which they tolerate hate speech (Hawdon et al., 2016). In the legal tradition of the US, free speech is protected under the Constitution and can only be regulated in specific, clearly defined circumstances. German law provides a contrast to the American approach. As specified in its Basic Law, Germany regulates and specifies punishments for general as well as specific forms of hate speech. In the UK, the Race Relations Act criminalises the intentional use of language that is likely to incite hatred against groups based on their colour, race or national origin. Finally, Finland has banned the expression of opinions by which a certain group is threatened, defamed or insulted on the basis of race, skin colour, birth status, national or ethnic origin or any comparable basis. These differences in legal frameworks affect the cultural and social norms of behaviour as individuals interact both online and offline.

Earlier research has also shown that the risk of exposure to different types of disturbing material varies by individuals' socio-demographic background and various behavioural characteristics. Figure 4.3 shows that this is also true when it comes to exposure to online hate. The figure shows the proportions of those exposed to online hate material by frequency of Internet use, living arrangements, age and gender. The proportions of exposure are combined for all the countries. The largest difference can be observed in terms of ICT activity. About 43 per cent of those who reported using the Internet several times a day had been exposed to online hate material, while the same was true of only 30 per cent of those who used the Internet less often. The difference is very significant ($p<0.001$). This shows that frequent online activity is an important factor associated with exposure to risk. Indeed, this is not a surprising finding given that spending time in a dangerous environment tends to increase the likelihood of negative experiences.

Furthermore, it has been noted for adults and young people alike that frequent Internet use is associated with general social activity both online and offline (e.g.

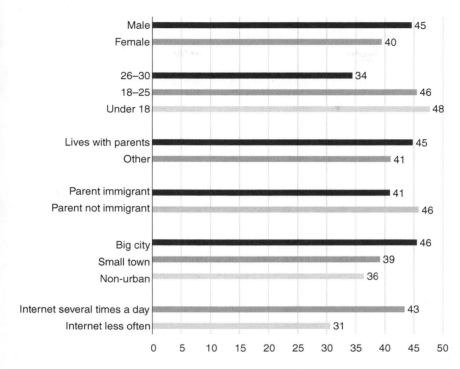

Figure 4.3 Exposure to online hate by respondents' background characteristics. Percentages.

Räsänen, 2008; van Dijk, 2005). Here, we can see that frequent use of the Internet is clearly an activity that increases the risk of exposure to hateful material. According to the general theoretical lines of Routine Activity Theory (see Chapter 3 above), people with wide social networks have a higher risk of being exposed to online hate. As the source of the risk here is other users, more access to others tends to increase the likelihood of encountering the work of negatively motivated users.

Additionally, in all four countries, males (44 per cent exposed) were more likely than females (40 per cent exposed) to encounter hate material online ($p<0.01$). However, the differences by age are even more visible. It is perhaps not surprising that the younger the online user, the more likely he or she is to encounter hateful material. At the same time, the difference between those who are over 26 and under 18 is significant ($p<0.001$). Approximately 34 per cent of respondents in the older age group reported exposure, while the proportion for the younger group is 47 per cent. The findings regarding age especially are in line with our general assumptions presented in earlier chapters of this book.

Similarly, Figure 4.3 indicates that respondents living with their parents (45 per cent exposed) were more likely to have witnessed hate material than those living independently (41 per cent exposed) ($p<0.05$). This is surprising given the fact that parents typically provide a level of guardianship to children. However, the size of the difference is only a few percentage points and among our sample it is the younger respondent group who have the highest risk of exposure. The difference is statistically significant ($p<0.05$). Needless to say, younger people also tend to live with their parents more often than do older ones. These findings show that some basic background characteristics are useful for understanding young people's risk of exposure to various online materials. In addition to these factors, place of residence has also been found to be associated with the risk of exposure to online hate (see Livingstone & Bovill, 2013; Näsi et al., 2015; Räsänen et al., 2016). Our findings also indicate that big city residents are more likely to see online hate content ($p<0.001$).

However, the previous information regarding exposure to online hate does not give us any information about what type of hate material young people are typically witnessing. As already discussed, it is possible that a particular type of hate material can be encountered more often in one country than in another. Political or religious issues, for instance, are discussed very differently across Europe. Therefore, the amount of hateful material targeting religious or political views can vary considerably cross-nationally. Our data give us the possibility to examine this issue. The questionnaires included the question: "Which of the following did the hateful or degrading material that you came across online relate to?" The question was followed by a list of ten different thematic topics, including sexual orientation, ethnicity and physical appearance. Table 4.2 shows the proportions of respondents who saw hate material about each topic. The percentages are shown for those who reported exposure to hateful or degrading materials, and not for the total samples.

As the table shows, in all four countries most hate material focused on sexual orientation and ethnicity. About 50 per cent or more of those who reported exposure to online hate said they had seen material targeted at these features. In Finland and the US, the proportions are over 60 per cent ($p<0.001$). This is not

Table 4.2 Exposure to different types of online hate content in the UK, the US, Germany and Finland. Percentages for those exposed to online hate

	UK	US	Germany	Finland
Sexual orientation	55	61	50	63
Ethnicity	57	60	48	67
Political views	31	48	36	29
Religious conviction/belief	43	45	44	40
Gender	44	44	20	25
Physical appearance	39	41	31	44
Physical disability	18	13	17	17
Terrorism	19	22	15	18
School shootings	10	21	6	9
General hatred of people	16	18	28	23

an unusual observation, since sexuality and ethnicity are more or less universal themes in daily discourse across the world. Political views were also relatively common targets of hate, although there were considerable differences by country ($p < 0.001$). In the US, 48 per cent of respondents said they had seen hate targeting political views, while in Germany the proportion was 36 per cent. The rate was about 30 per cent in both Finland and the UK. These findings related to politically charged hate can be viewed through the lens of American political culture, which is significantly more populist than that of the other of these countries. This can result in higher levels of division between members of opposing political parties. In political terms especially, it is argued that the US is different from many other Western countries, and even from the rest of the world (Lipset, 1997, pp. 34–35).

Hate material focused on gender was more often witnessed in the UK and US ($p < 0.001$). Over 40 per cent of British and American respondents had seen hateful material based on gender, compared with only about 20 per cent of Finnish and German respondents. This likely points to the fact that the incidence of gender-targeted hate content varies between countries. We must of course acknowledge that when dealing with national levels of exposure, comparative interpretations are never absolute and they can vary significantly on the basis of context. This is especially true for general issues, such as for material targeted at gender, ethnicity or appearance.

Hateful and degrading material that is not specifically targeted is relatively common. Material dealing with general hatred of people was witnessed by 28 per cent of the German respondents and 23 per cent of Finns. In the US and the UK, the proportion of those witnessing such material was below 20 per cent ($p < 0.001$). Perhaps connected to this, exposure to material on physical disability also varied only slightly among the countries, from 13 per cent (US) to 18 per cent (UK). Exposure to terrorism was slightly more common among the American and British respondents compared with the others. This is likely related to the primary role of the US and UK in the war against terror. However, the differences for the last two items are not statistically significant ($p > 0.05$).

Yet another variation between the countries has to do with material related to school shootings. In the US, hateful material targeting school shootings was witnessed by over 20 per cent of respondents, while fewer than 10 per cent saw this type of hate material in all other countries ($p < 0.001$). This finding is likely due to the fact that the US has witnessed more school shootings than any other nation in the world (Böckler, Seeger, Sitzer & Heitmeyer, 2013), with such incidents having increased during the 2000s (Blair & Schweit, 2014).

4.5 Hate takes new forms

Our data show that exposure to online hate material is common. This finding should be a red flag in the sense that the data show hate as a common part of the online experience that can carry negative effects. Online hate is often directed at specific types of persons, directly concerning physical appearance, gender, sexuality and religious and political beliefs. Online hatred also involves the dissemination of extremely violent material or material associated with terrorism and school shootings. The intent behind such content and the negative effects on the wellbeing of the users exposed represent a serious risk in the global online setting. In our data, hate takes a very personal form and is often directed at physical appearance, sexual orientation or gender. Here, the ramifications of exposure can be especially severe due to these characteristics being so closely tied to identity. Furthermore, as younger users tend to be more exposed, this represents a significant risk to the wellbeing of those in the key stages of social and psychological development in terms of both identity and self-image.

Online hate may also be quick to find new forms (see Williams & Burnap, 2015). People group together and organise quickly after societal changes, and social media facilitate this effectively. Existing organised hate groups are also eager to take advantage of economic insecurity or societal changes. The most recent results from Finland indicate that after the Paris terrorist attacks of November 2015 and mass immigration due to the Syria crisis, hate became more politicised and people reported seeing more online hate concerning ethnicity, religion and terrorism (Kaakinen, Oksanen & Räsänen, 2016). Hate can thus be specifically targeted at individual characteristics, or motivated by developments on a global scale relating to issues central to certain identity groups. This is just one example of how quickly international and domestic events can direct media discussions and have a consequent impact on the behaviour of social media users.

Our survey shows that exposure to online hate varies from country to country. We have already suggested that technological factors may help us to understand some of the differences, although each country may be considered advanced in terms of ICT usage. In addition, legislation might play a role, as mentioned, in terms of how hate content is punished in the countries surveyed. This carries weight in terms of differences in hate material targeting religion, where the varied legal ramifications involved may explain why the rates of exposure vary between countries. Additionally, some of the differences can also be explained by demographic and cultural factors, for example by ethnicity.

Online hate can harm us in many ways. People are easily influenced by emotional content and it is often the case that they rely on very basic reactions rather than rationality. Hate triggers what Nobel Prize winner Daniel Kahneman (2011) has called System 1 thinking, which is fast, automatic and emotional. People react to anger with anger, rather than by using System 2 thinking, which is slow, logical and conscious. Hence, we react before we think about what we are saying. This very emotionality keeps the engine of social media going. Studies show that negativity is the fuel of online conversations (Chmiel et al., 2011, 2014). When fast and irrational System 1 thinking is combined with social-psychological factors affecting group behaviour, we begin to understand how hate escalates and only leads to more anger.

The expressed negative emotions and hate have no positive consequences. The current body of literature does not support the idea of cathartic aggression (i.e. letting off steam) (Bushman, 2002). Entire websites called rant sites are devoted to venting off. Martin and colleagues (2013) set up two studies on visitors to rant sites and found that they were more angry than other people, and expressed their anger in maladaptive ways, reading and writing rants being associated with negative shifts in mood. Despite the potential benefits such sites may have in the short term as a way for some individuals to let off steam, longer-term effects point to negative impacts on wellbeing. Furthermore, angry and hateful online users may easily disturb the online activity of dozens or even hundreds of other users without having to face any consequences for their actions.

References

Arts, W., & Gelissen, J. (2002). Three worlds of welfare capitalism or more? A state-of-the-art report. *Journal of European Social Policy, 12*(2), 137–158. DOI: 10.1177/0952 872002012002114.

Banks, J. (2011). European regulation of cross-border hate speech in cyberspace: The limits of legislation. *European Journal of Crime, Criminal Law and Criminal Justice, 19*(1), 1–13. DOI: 10.1163/157181711X553933.

Barbosa, N., & Faria, A. P. (2011). Innovation across Europe: How important are institutional differences? *Research Policy, 40*(9), 1157–1169. DOI: 10.1016/j.respol.2011. 05.017.

Berlet, C. (2001, April). When hate went online. In *Northeast Sociological Association Spring Conference in April* (pp. 1–20). Retrieved from http://citeseerx.ist.psu.edu/ viewdoc/download?doi=10.1.1.552.239&rep=rep1&type=pdf.

Blair, J. P., & Schweit, K. W. (2014). *A Study of Active Shooter Incidents, 2000–2013*. Texas State University and Federal Bureau of Investigation, US Department of Justice, Washington DC. Retrieved from www.fbi.gov/about-us/office-of-partner-engagement/active-shooter-incidents/a-study-of-active-shooter-incidents-in-the-u.s.-2000-2013.

Blazak, R. (2009). Toward a working definition of hate groups. In B. Perry, B. Levin, P. Iganski, R. Blazak & F. Lawrence (Eds.), *Hate Crimes* (pp. 133–162). Westport, CT: Greenwood Publishing Group.

Bowman-Grieve, L. (2009) Exploring "stormfront": A virtual community of the radical right. *Studies in Conflict & Terrorism, 32*(11), 989–1007. DOI: 10.1080/1057610 0903259951.

Brown, C. (2009). WWW.HATE.COM: White supremacist discourse on the Internet and the construction of whiteness ideology. *Howard Journal of Communications, 20*(2), 189–208. DOI: 10.1080/10646170902869544.

Brown, R. (2011). *Prejudice: Its Social Psychology*. Chichester: John Wiley & Sons.

Burris, V., Smith, E., & Strahm, A. (2000). White supremacist networks on the Internet. *Sociological Focus, 33*(2), 215–235. DOI: 10.1080/00380237.2000.10571166.

Bushman, B. J. (2002). Does venting anger feed or extinguish the flame? Catharsis, rumination, distraction, anger, and aggressive responding. *Personality and Social Psychology Bulletin, 28*(6), 724–731. DOI: 10.1177/0146167202289002.

Böckler, N., Seeger, T., Sitzer, P., & Heitmeyer, W. (2013). School shootings: Conceptual framework and international empirical trends. In N. Böckler, S. Thorsten, P. Sitzer & W. Heitmeyer (Eds.), *School Shootings: International Research, Case Studies and Concepts for Prevention* (pp. 1–24). New York: Springer. DOI: 10.1007/978-1-4614-5526-4_1.

Chau, M., & Xu, J. (2007). Mining communities and their relationships in blogs: A study of hate groups. *International Journal of Human-Computer Studies, 65*(1), 57–70. DOI: 10.1016/j.ijhcs.2006.08.009.

Chmiel, A., Sienkiewicz, J., Thelwall, M., Paltoglou, G., Buckley, K., Kappas, A., & Hołyst, J. A. (2011). Collective emotions online and their influence on community life. *PloS one, 6*(7), e22207. DOI: 10.1371/journal.pone.0022207.

Chmiel, A., Sienkiewicz, J., Paltoglou, G., Buckley, K., Skowron, M., Thelwall, M. et al. (2014) Collective emotions online. In N. Agarwal, M. Lim & R. T. Wigand (Eds.), *Online Collective Action* (pp. 59–74). Vienna: Springer. DOI: 10.1093/acprof:oso/9780 199659180.001.0001.

Citron, D. K. (2014). *Hate Crimes in Cyberspace*. Cambridge, MA: Harvard University Press.

Citron, D. K., & Norton, H. (2011). Intermediaries and hate speech: Fostering digital citizenship for our information age. *Boston University Law Review, 91*(4), 1435–1484. Retrieved from http://ssrn.com/abstract=1764004.

Council of Europe (2013). *Young People Combating Hate Speech Online*. Campaign of Young People for Human Rights Online 2012–2014. Retrieved from www. nohatespeechmovement.org/campaign.

Craig, W., Harel-Fisch, Y., Fogel-Grinvald, H., Dostaler, S., Hetland, J., Simons-Morton, B. et al. (2009). A cross-national profile of bullying and victimisation among adolescents in 40 countries. *International Journal of Public Health, 54*(2), 216–224. DOI: 10.1007/s00038-009-5413-9.

Currie, C., Gabhainn, S. N., Godeau, E., Roberts, C., Smith, R., Currie, D., & Barnekow, V. (Eds.) (2008). *Inequalities in Young People's Health: HBSC International Report from the 2005/2006 Survey*. Copenhagen: WHO Regional Office for Europe.

Douglas, K. M. (2007). Psychology, discrimination and hate groups online. In A. Joinson, K. McKenna, T. Postmes & U.-D. Reips (Eds.), *The Oxford Handbook of Internet Psychology* (pp. 155–164). Oxford: Oxford University Press.

Elgar, F. J., McKinnon, B., Walsh, S. D., Freeman, J., Donnelly, P. D., de Matos, M. G. et al. (2015). Structural determinants of youth bullying and fighting in 79 countries. *Journal of Adolescent Health, 57*(6), 643–650. DOI: 10.1016/S0140-6736(14)61460-4.

Esping-Andersen, G. (1993). *Changing Classes: Stratification and Mobility in Post-Industrial Societies*. London: Sage.

European Commission against Racism and Intolerance (ECRI) (2016). *ECRI General Policy Recommendation No. 15 on Combating Hate Speech*. Strasbourg: Council of Europe. Retrieved from www.coe.int/t/dghl/monitoring/ecri/activities/GPR/EN/ Recommendation_N15/REC-15-2016-015-ENG.pdf.

Foxman, A. H., & Wolf, C. (2013). *Viral Hate: Containing Its Spread on the Internet*. London: Palgrave Macmillan.

Franklin, R. (2002). The hate directory. Retrieved from http://gse.buffalo.edu/fas/ bromley/classes/confres/hatedir.pdf.

Gerstenfeld, P. B. (2013). *Hate Crimes: Causes, Controls, and Controversies*. London: Sage.

Hawdon, J., Oksanen, A., & Räsänen, P. (2014). Victims of online groups: American youth's exposure to online hate speech. In J. Hawdon, J. Ryan & M. Lucht (Eds.), *The Causes and Consequences of Group Violence: From Bullies to Terrorists* (pp. 165–182). Lanham, MD: Lexington Books and Rowman & Littlefield.

Hawdon, J., Oksanen, A., & Räsänen, P. (2016). Exposure to online hate in four nations: A cross-national consideration. *Deviant Behavior, 37* (forthcoming).

HelHO:2012:1. Decision of the Supreme Court of Helsinki in Finland. Retrieved from www.oikeus.fi/hovioikeudet/helsinginhovioikeus/fi/index/hovioikeusratkaisut/hovioikeusratkaisut/1323295200099.html.

Internet Live Stats (2014). Retrieved from www.Internetlivestats.com/Internet-users-by-country/.

Jones, L. M., Mitchell, K. J., & Finkelhor, D. (2012). Trends in youth Internet victimization: Findings from three youth Internet safety surveys 2000–2010. *Journal of Adolescent Health, 50*(2), 179–186. DOI: 10.1016/j.jadohealth.2011.09.015.

Jones, L. M., Mitchell, K. J., & Finkelhor, D. (2013). Online harassment in context: Trends from three youth Internet safety surveys (2000, 2005, 2010). *Psychology of Violent, 3*(1), 53.

Kaakinen, M., Oksanen, A., & Räsänen, P. (2016). How did the Paris terrorist attacks change hate content in social media? (article manuscript).

Kaakinen, M., Oksanen, A., Keipi, T., Näsi, M., Minkkinen, J., & Räsänen, P. (2016). Associations between online hate content production and offline and online cognitive social capital (article manuscript).

Kahneman, D. (2011). *Thinking, Fast and Slow*. London: Macmillan.

Kiesler, S., Siegel, J., & McGuire, T. W. (1984). Social psychological aspects of computer-mediated communication. *American Psychologist, 39*(10), 1123–1134. DOI: 10.1037/0003-066X.39.10.1123.

Kvist, J., Fritzell, J., Hvinden, B., & Kangas, O. (Eds.) (2012). *Changing Social Equality: The Nordic Welfare Model in the 21st Century*. Bristol: Policy Press.

Lee, E., & Leets, L. (2002). Persuasive storytelling by hate groups online. *American Behavioral Scientist, 45*(6), 927–957. DOI: 10.1177/0002764202045006003.

Levin, B. (2002). Cyberhate: A legal and historical analysis of extremists' use of computer networks in America. *American Behavioral Scientist, 45*(6), 958–988. DOI: 10.1177/0002764202045006004.

Lipset, S. M. (1997). *American Exceptionalism: A Double-Edged Sword*. New York: W. W. Norton.

Livingstone, S. & Bovill, M. (Eds.) (2013). *Children and their Changing Media Environment: A European Comparative Study*. New York: Routledge.

Livingstone, S., Haddon, L., Görzig, A., & Ólafsson, K. (2011). *Risks and Safety on the Internet: The Perspective of European Children. Full findings of EU Kids Online*. London: LSE.

Martin, R. C., Coyier, K. R., VanSistine, L. M., & Schroeder, K. L. (2013). Anger on the Internet: The perceived value of rant-sites. *Cyberpsychology, Behaviour, and Social Networking, 16*(2), 119–122. DOI: 10.1089/cyber.2012.0130.

Mishra, R. (2014). *Welfare State Capitalist Society*. London: Routledge.

Näsi, M. J., Oksanen, A., Keipi, T., & Räsänen, P. (2015). Cybercrime victimization among young people: A multi-national study. *Journal of Scandinavian Studies in Criminology and Crime Prevention, 16*(2), 203–2010. 10.1080/14043858.2015.1046640.

Näsi, M., Räsänen, P., Oksanen, A., Hawdon, J., Keipi, T., & Holkeri, E. (2014). Association between online harassment and exposure to harmful online content: A cross-national comparison between the United States and Finland. *Computers in Human Behavior, 41*(December), 137–145. DOI: 10.1016/j.chb.2014.09.019.

Oksanen, A., Räsänen, P., & Hawdon, J. (2014). Hate Groups: From offline to online social identifications. In J. Hawdon, J. Ryan & M. Lucht (Eds.), *The Causes and Consequences of Group Violence: From Bullies to Terrorists* (pp. 21–47). Lanham, MD: Lexington Books and Rowman & Littlefield.

74   *The rise of online hate*

Oksanen, A., Hawdon, J., Holkeri, E., Näsi, M., & Räsänen, P. (2014). Exposure to online hate among young social media users. *Sociological Studies of Children & Youth, 18*, 253–273. DOI: 10.1108/S1537-466120140000018021.

Potok, M. (2015) The year in hate and extremism. Intelligence report. Southern Poverty Law Center, US. Retrieved from www.splcenter.org/fighting-hate/intelligence-report/2015/year-hate-and-extremism-0.

Potok, M. (2016) The Year in Hate and Extremism. Intelligence report. Southern Poverty Law Center, US. Retrieved from www.splcenter.org/fighting-hate/intelligence-report/2016/year-hate-and-extremism.

Pöyhtäri, R., Haara, P., & Raittila, P. (2013). *Vihapuhe sanavapautta kaventamassa.* Tampere: Tampere University Press.

Reyns, B. W., Henson, B., & Fisher, B. S. (2011). Being pursued online: Applying cyberlifestyle-routine activities theory to cyberstalking victimization. *Criminal Justice and Behavior, 38*, 1149–1169. DOI: 10.1177/0093854811421448.

Räsänen, P. (2006). Information society for all? Structural characteristics of Internet use in 15 European countries. *European Societies, 8*(1), 59–81. DOI: 10.1080/146166905 00491423.

Räsänen, P. (2008). The aftermath of the ICT revolution? Media and communication technology preferences in Finland in 1999 and 2004. *New Media & Society, 10*(2), 225–245. DOI: 10.1177/1461444807086471.

Räsänen, P., Hawdon, J., Holkeri, E., Näsi, M., Keipi, T., & Oksanen, A. (2016). Targets of online hate: Examining determinants of victimization among young Finnish Facebook users. *Violence & Victims, 31*(4). DOI: 10.1891/0886-6708.VV-D-14–00079.

SSI (2016). Data solutions and technology for market researchers. Retrieved from www.surveysampling.com/about/.

Tajfel, H. (1970). Experiments in intergroup discrimination. *Scientific American, 223*, 96–102. Retrieved from https://asfranthompson.files.wordpress.com/2011/11/tajfel-1970-experiments-in-intergroup-discrimination.pdf.

Van Dijk, J. A. G. M. (2005). *The Deepening Divide: Inequality in the Information Society.* Thousand Oaks, CA: SAGE Publications.

Waldron, J. (2012). *The Harm in the Hate Speech.* Cambridge, MA: Harvard University Press.

Wall, D. (2001). Cybercrimes and the Internet. In D. Wall (Ed.), *Crime and the Internet* (pp. 1–17). New York: Routledge.

Williams, M. L., & Burnap, P. (2015). Cyberhate on social media in the aftermath of Woolwich: A case study in computational criminology and big data. *British Journal of Criminology.* First published online (25 June 2015). DOI: 10.1093/bjc/azv059.

World Internet Statistics. (2016). Retrieved from www.internetlivestats.com/internet-users-by-country/.

5 Impacts of online hate

5.1 Potentially harmful or always harmful?

The previous chapter examined exposure to online hate at a very general level, through teenagers' and young adults' exposure to hateful or degrading material. These observations relate to the possible consequences of exposure to hate. We proposed that exposure to hate and especially personal victimisation by hate leads to negative outcomes, posing a serious threat to the subjective wellbeing and happiness of young people (Proctor, Linley & Maltby, 2009).

Given that there is a potentially vast amount of online content that can be perceived as negative or harmful, it is necessary to systematically examine how often young people actually see this type of material in order for us to form an idea of the extent of exposure to hate online. While numerous scholars and activists note the potential dangers of the widespread availability of online hate materials (e.g. Foxman & Wolf, 2013; Waldron, 2012), few have investigated how, and how often, young people become victimised by cyberhate. Moreover, we need a comparative perspective to evaluate the situation in Europe. International comparison is important, as while the Internet offers a relatively homogeneous communication environment for individuals, the existing patterns of Internet use vary greatly from one country to another (e.g. Livingstone & Helsper, 2010; Räsänen, 2008).

Online hate involves both indirect and direct harm. Indirect social harm raises possible ethical and legal questions as to whether the dissemination of hate material should be allowed in society (Waldron, 2012). Content that proposes direct harm may cause socially and psychologically damaging effects at both personal and group levels (Leets & Giles, 1997; Tynes, 2006). For example, the long-term effects of exposure to hateful online material may include reinforcing discrimination against vulnerable groups (Foxman & Wolf, 2013). As a result, victims may develop defensive and hyper-vigilant attitudes that can potentially be dangerous, lasting for months or even years (Leets, 2002).

Preceding studies suggest that personal victimisation by different forms of online hate is also relatively common, especially among young people. Considerable research has been conducted into various forms of online victimisation, including online grooming (Whittle, Hamilton-Giachritsis, Beech & Collings,

2013), online harassment (Bossler, Holt & May, 2012; Jones, Mitchell & Finkelhor, 2013; Näsi et al., 2014), cybercrime (Näsi, Räsänen, Hawdon, Holkeri & Oksanen, 2015; Oksanen & Keipi, 2013), and especially cyberbullying (Helweg-Larsen, Schütt & Larsen, 2012; Sourander et al., 2010; Tokunaga, 2010). Here, the examination of the implications of negative content and behaviour raises questions around wellbeing, social trust, self-image and social relations. Our analysis here focuses on the associations between online hate and certain demographic variables in order to determine at-risk groups.

5.2 Victimisation by hate, harassment and crime online

Before turning to the consequences of exposure to online hate, we need to determine how common personal victimisation by negative online behaviour really is. In our questionnaires we examined online victimisation through three different items measuring cyberhate, cybercrime and cyberharassment. First, the respondents were asked whether or not they had personally been the target of hateful or degrading material online. The second item was concerned with whether or not they had been a target of harassment online (for example, whether people had spread private or groundless information about them or shared pictures of them without permission). The third item measured whether or not someone had had a crime committed against them online in the past three years.

Figure 5.1 shows that personal victimisation by cyberhate is clearly less common in Germany (with only 4 per cent) than in the US (15 per cent), the UK (12 per cent) and Finland (10 per cent) ($p < 0.001$). These differences are notable despite the Internet user penetration rates being very high in each of the four

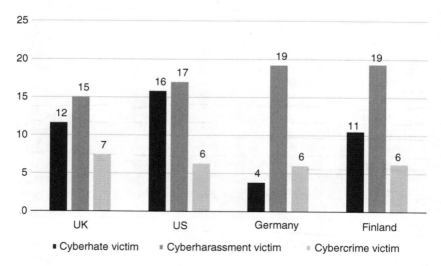

Figure 5.1 Victimisation by cyberhate, cybercrime and cyberharassment in the UK, the US, Germany and Finland. Percentages.

countries. The English language may play a role here in addition to other socio-cultural factors. We return to this issue later on in the chapter. The differences between rates of victimisation by cyberharassment and cybercrime are clearly smaller. Cyberharassment was relatively common in the four countries with rates of victimisation ranging from 15 per cent in the UK to 19 per cent in Germany and Finland. Victimisation by cybercrime was not as common as victimisation by hate or harassment online. Figures for cybervictimisation range from 6 per cent in Germany to 7 per cent in the UK. Hence, the cross-country differences are marginal for cyberharassment and cybercrime.

The findings regarding personal victimisation clearly contrast with the findings related to exposure to online hate. Although many users were exposed to online hate, only some became targeted victims. We were therefore interested in examining the reasons for this victimisation. For this purpose, our questionnaires listed a total of eight types of motives, ranging from ethnicity or nationality to sexual orientation, political views and appearance. In Figure 5.2 we show the reasons for cyberhate victimisation by country.

Figure 5.2 shows that, for victims of cyberhate, appearance was the most common reason for victimisation in all four countries. The percentage was highest in Finland and lowest in the UK, as 50 per cent of Finns and 38 per cent of British were victimised based on their appearance. The percentages were 42 for Germans and 43 for Americans. Although the importance of appearance has been widely discussed in recent studies on consumption and lifestyle

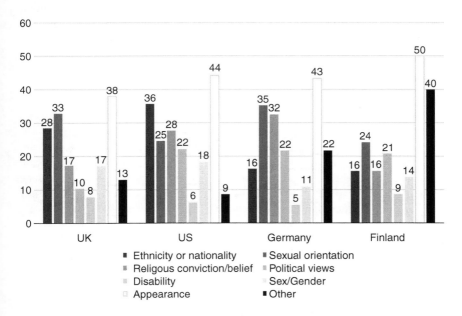

Figure 5.2 The reasons of cyberhate victimisation. Percentages for those who have been personally victimised in the UK, the US, Germany and Finland.

(e.g. Grogan, 2007; Sarpila, 2014), empirical studies on social media use have not previously delved into how widespread a phenomenon appearance-related hate material actually is. Appearance-related targeting is just one of the examples of how hate can be very personal and subjective. This is a significant issue, particularly since younger users value self-presentation, seeking validation through selfies and in their use of photo-sharing platforms such as Instagram (Kim, Lee, Sung & Choi, 2016). Through creating visual material of themselves to attract attention, young people expose themselves as targets of potential criticism, insults, bullying and various other forms of hateful messages.

In terms of the other reasons for cyberhate, the results varied greatly between the countries. In Germany and the UK, sexual orientation was the second most common reason for victimisation (in Germany 35 per cent, in the UK 32 per cent). In the US, the second most common reason for hate victimisation was ethnicity or nationality (36 per cent). Finland was somewhat of an exception here, as the second most common reason for victimisation was content categorised as "some other than any listed types". Almost 40 per cent of those victimised by cyberhate in Finland disclosed that the reason for their victimisation related to something not in the listed categories. Besides appearance, other similarities were also prevalent cross-nationally. Disability and sex/gender were among the least common reasons for cyberhate victimisation in each of the four countries, with less than 10 per cent of respondents listing them.

Overall, personal victimisation was relatively common in terms of our comparative data, indicating that hateful material is quite often targeted at Internet users personally. This of course raises additional questions on the nature of social media and other computer-mediated communication, one such question being: how do the different forms of hate victimisation really affect respondents' wellbeing?

5.3 Impacts on wellbeing

Past research has shown that exposure to hate material and experiences of victimisation are associated with negative consequences. For example, sleeping disorders, increased anxiety and feelings of fear and insecurity can result from cybercrime, hate victimisation or other forms of online harassment. In addition to negative psychological outcomes and even psychiatric symptoms, online hate has been found to affect people's daily activities and the ways in which they relate to their surrounding environment (e.g. Lee & Leets, 2002; Näsi et al., 2015).

In the social sciences, there are various traditions for understanding and conceptualising people's wellbeing. There are a number of definitions of physical, mental and social wellbeing. Views differ as to their theoretical and methodological foundations (e.g. Diener & Seligman, 2004; Veenhoven, 2010). For example, some prefer to stress the role of material or economic components whereas others see them as more cultural or psychological effects. In addition, contrary views have been presented as to whether wellbeing should serve as a predictor rather than as an outcome. The question therefore is: does perceived wellbeing result primarily from certain life conditions and activities or should wellbeing be seen as something that can explain people's activities and life patterns?

Research on quality of life and wellbeing relies primarily on three different traditions, namely the socio-psychological, the economic and the ecological traditions. According to Schuessler and Fisher (1985), for instance, in social psychological approaches, quality of life and wellbeing are normally associated with experiencing happiness, contentment and other subjectively described conditions. These subjective conditions are achieved through the satisfaction of physiological and social needs, as well as those needs connected with self-realisation. In the economic tradition, on the other hand, emphasis is put on the rational nature of an individual's actions. The pursuit of quality of life and wellbeing are seen as means by which rational actors may obtain the most significant utilities possible from available resources. Finally, the ecological approach differs from the social psychological and economic traditions as it foregrounds the effect of an individual's physical environment and social circumstances. In this approach, experiences of wellbeing are defined as resulting from different situational factors, such as day-to-day social interactions and routines.

Many alternative but relatively similar classifications of research traditions have been presented in the literature (e.g. Diener, 2000; Veenhoven, 2010). What is considered important are the different dimensions of wellbeing and quality of life, because the meaning of wellbeing can vary from one occasion to another. In our study, we were primarily interested in impacts on subjective wellbeing (SWB). As discussed above, SWB has been used in sociological, psychological and economic research in the identification of such issues as differences in experienced standard of living, enjoyment of life, life satisfaction and happiness. A high level of life satisfaction or happiness, for instance, offers positively evaluated descriptions of an individual's situation. However, there has never been a consensus in the social sciences on the most effective measures of wellbeing, despite agreement on important components (e.g. Etzioni, 1968; Kouvo & Räsänen, 2015; Veenhoven, 2010, 2012). Here, we examine SWB through all of its most widely used dimensions:

- happiness (general dimension)
- economic condition (economic dimension)
- trust (interpersonal dimension) and
- self-esteem (psychological dimension).

The four listed dimensions capture all of the essential components of wellbeing. In the literature on SWB there are several partially contradictory research traditions. In empirical studies, however, different dimensions of SWB are often used interchangeably. Here, the four dimensions are used to capture the qualitative evaluation of an individual's current life situation. Happiness was measured by widely applied question: "All things considered, how happy would you say you are?" The economic dimension was evaluated by the question: "At the moment, how satisfied are you with your own economic situation?" Our measure of inter-personal trust was based on the question: "Would you say that the following people can be trusted, or that you can't be too careful in dealing with these people?" Those listed were people in general, family members, good friends, work colleagues and other acquaintances. Finally, self-esteem was based on the Single-Item Self-Esteem Scale, namely through the indicator, "I have high self-esteem" (Robins, Hendin & Trzesniewski, 2001).

Each of the items was originally measured on a ten-point scale (1 = "extremely unhappy/dissatisfied/not true of me" and 10 = "extremely happy/satisfied/very true of me"). Since our data come from a cross-sectional study, we cannot say very much about the direction of the effects. However, we discuss the effects of exposure to hate rather than the effects of SWB. We will return to this issue in more detail towards the end of the chapter.

According to a recent study, even witnessing hate material online resulted in lowered levels of happiness and life satisfaction among young Internet users (Näsi et al., 2015). However, in order to examine the association between SWB and hate victimisation more closely, we took into account the type of negative behaviour that the respondents were targeted by. We examine how cyberhate, cyberharassment and cybercrime victimisation are associated with different dimensions of SWB. Given that the rates of victimisation differ substantially among the studied countries, we examine them separately, beginning with the issue of cybercrime victimisation. Figure 5.3 shows the averages (on a scale from 1 to 10) for those who have been targets of hateful or degrading material and those who have not.

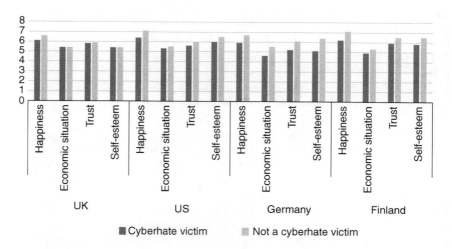

Figure 5.3 Victimisation by cyberhate and its association with wellbeing in the UK, the US, Germany and Finland. Means (evaluated on a scale from 1 to 10).

As the figure shows, the levels are lower for all dimensions of SWB for those who have been victimised by cyberhate. This finding is consistent cross-nationally, despite the fact that the overall levels of wellbeing as well as related effects tend to vary from one country to another. The most notable differences emerge when we compare levels of happiness and self-esteem. Those who have not been victimised by cyberhate reported higher levels of happiness in all countries ($p<0.05$). The effects are strongest in Finland ($p<0.01$) and the US ($p<0.001$). The same can be said about self-esteem, except in the case of the UK, which showed no differences. Furthermore, trust is lower in all countries among those who have been victims, although the difference is not statistically significant in the UK.

In addition, we must note that in the UK, the US and Finland there were no major differences in terms of economic situation, while in Germany ($p<0.05$) victims reported lower economic satisfaction. This may be due to the fact that the economic dimension of SWB is not the first aspect affected by cyberhate victimisation. Here, economic situation is a background condition, which helps individuals orient themselves for future life events and forthcoming decisions. In addition, it has been shown that satisfaction with one's economic situation is also associated with broader societal factors, such as inflation or unemployment rates (Dolan, Peasgood & White, 2008). Nevertheless, economic wellbeing has significance for all our daily experiences and our findings show that personal victimisation by cyberhate associates negatively with economic satisfaction.

Figure 5.4 shows the results for cyberharassment. Again, it appears that happiness has the most notable association with harassment experiences in the US, Germany and Finland ($p<0.001$). The UK is clearly an exception, however, since the levels of SWB do not appear to vary at all between those who have experienced online harassment and those who have not. Our data do not allow us to

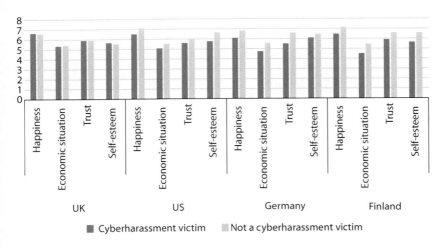

Figure 5.4 Victimisation by cyberharassment and its associations with wellbeing in the UK, the US, Germany and Finland. Means (evaluated on a scale from 1 to 10).

make strong interpretations as to why cyberharassment has only marginal impacts on different dimensions of SWB in the UK. But in the other countries, those who had been harassed reported lower scores than those who had not had such experiences ($p<0.05$). In addition to happiness, harassed respondents reported far lower self-esteem and satisfaction with their economic situation than others in the US, Germany and Finland. Similar differences also exist in terms of trust.

Finally, Figure 5.5 shows the mean ratings of SWB among those who have been cybercrime victims and those who have not. We see that in Finland the differences between cybercrime victims and those who are not victims are the most significant, whereas they are more moderate in the US and Germany. In interpreting these findings, we again need to bear in mind that the questionnaires mentioned the past three years, which is a relatively long period of time. It should be noted, however, that cybercrime victimisation is often a somewhat different experience from cyberharassment or cyberhate victimisation. This fact is likely reflected in the findings as well.

Figure 5.5 also shows that happiness is affected by cybercrime victimisation in all the countries. The effects are very strong in Finland ($p<0.001$) and Germany ($p<0.001$), and somewhat weaker in the US ($p<0.05$). In the UK, cybercrime victims reported lower happiness though the difference is not statistically significant. We also observe interesting differences when comparing the results by countries and by the four dimensions of SWB. For instance, we see that levels of trust are lower among the victims in Finland ($p<0.001$) and Germany ($p<0.05$). Findings also indicate that cybercrime victimisation has a negative impact on young people's self-esteem. We observe this across the samples, except for the UK. The overall finding does not come as a surprise, given that criminal activities can be the most insulting expressions of hate that one can be targeted by.

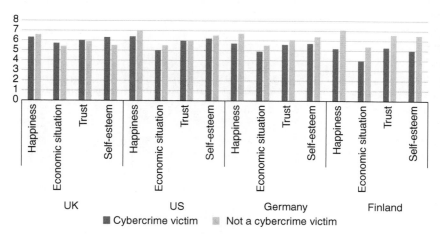

Figure 5.5 Cybercrime victimisation and its association with wellbeing in the UK, the US, Germany and Finland. Means (evaluated on a scale from 1 to 10).

In Finland ($p<0.01$), Germany and the US, those who have been victimised by cybercrime expressed lower levels of economic satisfaction. In the UK, there is a weak difference which shows that economic satisfaction is lower for those who have not been victimised. However, the difference in the UK is only marginal and not statistically significant. Again, we cannot be sure about the direction of effects, but the results are clear: cybercrime victimisation is associated with different dimensions of SWB among the studied teenagers and young adults.

5.4 Associations between personal victimisation and social relations

In this final section we examine how cyberhate victimisation connects with general offline and online activity. As discussed in Chapter 3, Lifestyle Exposure Theory (LET) and Routine Activity Theory (RAT) provide us with strong indicators of which behavioural and environmental factors are associated with the risk of cybervictimisation. The basic argument in existing online studies is that traditional settings for victimisation, such as homes, restaurants or nightclubs, and workplaces, have been extended to include various online environments (e.g. Bossler & Holt, 2009; Holt, Bossler & May, 2012; Räsänen et al., 2016).

As they do in the offline context, young individuals use the online space following certain routines, for instance by checking their social media profiles regularly, participating in online discussion forums related to their interests, looking for news and information from their regular sources, as well as, on occasion, seeking out new content. However, despite these daily online routines, users may also come across some online material by accident, entering websites with content they did not intend to be exposed to. In some cases, such accidental exposure reveals content that is hostile and harmful; or, worse, online behaviour can result in a person becoming a victim of actual crime. Despite being in a relatively different environment, individuals' offline activities also continue to be significant predictors of online victimisation, as negative offline networks can influence alternative leisure activities and potentially harmful and even dangerous online routines (Helweg-Larsen, Schütt & Larsen, 2012; Räsänen et al., 2016).

A key notion of RAT is that routine activities are a universal source of risk factors and potential victimisation. That is, when all relevant background factors are accounted for, it is routine activity that eventually explains who is most at risk of becoming a victim of crime, converging in time and space with an offender and lacking appropriate measures of protection. In this sense, routine activities can explain cybervictimisation in different contexts and among different population groups in a rather uniform manner. Because of this broad applicability of the risk setting combined with an activity level that is shared in online experience cross-nationally, we do not delve into cross-national differences in this context. Here, the question arises: how well can young people's Internet use patterns and meeting offline friends explain their risk of becoming victims of cyberhate?

In our data, we examined users' Internet use frequency as the online activity measure. That is, the item measured how often they log on. Similarly, social activity was measured using a widely applied item formulated as "How often do you meet face to face with friends, relatives or work colleagues for social reasons?" In the analysis, we compared levels of socialisation between those who report meeting friends/relatives/colleagues less than once a month and those who report meeting with friends/relatives/colleagues at least once a month.

Our findings do not indicate clearly that more active users of the Internet are more likely to become victims of cybercrime. However, this is because 90 per cent of our respondents were using the Internet several times a day, thus a more detailed measurement of daily Internet use might provide more detailed findings through producing a valuable contrast. For instance, our question concerning respondents' social media activity allows for a more detailed examination. In our data, social media use was measured by asking respondents to identify which from a list of twenty-one different social media services (e.g. Facebook, Twitter, Google+, YouTube, message and image boards, photo-sharing services) they were using. The results show that respondents who used more sites or services were more likely to be victims of cybercrime, cyberharassment and cyberhate.

However, we also found that respondents' offline activities tend to have an association with cybercrime and cyberhate victimisation. This association shows that respondents who were meeting their friends, relatives or colleagues face to face on social occasions less than once a month were more likely to become victims than those making social connections more often. However, cyberharrasment victimisation was not associated with offline activity. Approximately 11 per cent of those who met their friends, relatives or colleagues for social occasions on less than a monthly basis had become victims of a cybercrime during the past three years. The proportion of victimised respondents is 6 per cent for those who met their friends, relatives or colleagues more often ($p < 0.001$). Similarly, about 15 per cent of those who reported meeting with friends, relatives or colleagues less often than once a month had become victims of cyberhate. The proportion is clearly lower (10 per cent) for those who met with friends more often ($p < 0.01$).

In terms of percentages, there appear to be only slight associations between meeting friends, relatives or colleagues and cyberhate victimisation. However, in broader terms, it is plausible that social activities both online and offline are associated with the likelihood of victimisation online. For instance, it has been found that while frequency of social connections seems to reduce the risk of victimisation, frequent use of the Internet increases risk (e.g. Bossler et al., 2012; Räsänen et al., 2016). Such findings are important for young people, due to the fact that of all demographic groups in Western societies, it is young people who spend the most time online. Thus, the positive relationship between the risks linked to victimisation and the quantity of time spent online can be well understood given this assumption.

5.5 Often harmful, always disturbing

While examining whether the Internet serves as a homogenising environment for experiences of victimisation, we must acknowledge how the four countries in our study compare in the offline context. While we lack the data to statistically explore potential explanations for these cross-national differences, we can offer some plausible hypotheses that future research might investigate in more depth. Effects of cross-national variation in crime rates and cross-national differences in anti-hate speech laws might be feasible points of departure here. Consequently, our findings may in part be explained by the differences in hate speech laws in these countries. At least some of the variation in findings would benefit from a closer look at the institutional perspective. Each of the countries included is different in terms of the content that resulted in personal victimisation by cyberhate and also in terms of how victimisation was associated with wellbeing.

Part of our findings can also be explained by the fact that young people in non-English-speaking countries do not necessarily have access to English-language sites. On the other hand, Finnish users, who come from a small language group (just over 5 million speakers) are more likely to need the English language for online navigation than, for example, Germans (over 90 million speakers). This is especially relevant when it comes to cross-country differences in exposure and victimisation to different forms of online hate. Naturally, the boundaries that come with language also connect with cultural and legal factors, which vary between the countries. The lower rates of exposure to hate and victimisation in Germany might also be explained by stricter controls on online material.

Furthermore, the potential harms and dangers of cybervictimisation are not likely to impact all young people in similar ways. First, the highest risk group is made up of those young people who already face various difficulties and have experienced victimisation offline (Noll et al., 2013). They may also have fewer resources to cope with negative experiences online. Second, there is recent research evidence showing that primary groups may shield young people's mental health when they encounter online risks (Minkkinen et al., 2016). In other words, if adolescents have good friendships and good relationships with their parents, they are less likely to be impacted by negative online experiences.

All of this points to the fact that the sources of problems do not lie solely online (Mitchell et al., 2011). Obviously, it is difficult to control all potential risks resulting from Internet use; in fact, it may be easier to reduce online risks by addressing various contextual offline factors. For example, online victimisation has been shown to associate with low levels of attachment to family (Oksanen et al., 2014). Similarly, the psychosocial problems that young people confront offline overlap with their negative online experiences. It is therefore critical to develop new ways for parents, teachers and youth workers to support young people and address the identity issues they face. In addition, we need open discussions about the high prevalence of aggressive, hateful and threatening online behaviour. Only by confronting it can we hope to address the potential harm it may inflict.

Media literacy *important* [handwritten margin notes]

Media literacy also plays a very important role, much as it has in the offline setting where reading and interpretation become central to managing reactions to various forms of content. In Western societies it is no longer an exaggeration to argue that online skills are becoming a new source of socio-economic inequality. Being able to identify the different forms of online material and how they relate to different ideologies will be an increasingly important factor when considering the future of younger generations and their online proficiency linked to well-being. Visual information will have an increasingly significant role in how young people are exposed to content, especially for those where video, images and other signs are virtually ever present via various forms of social media. Suicide, violence, weight control issues and pornography are all part of this context, carrying increasing significance in the visual arena online in affecting the development of exposed users. Furthermore, while empirical research on the impacts and consequences of online hate is accumulating, we should note that the online environment and its widely used applications are also evolving quickly. It follows that many suggestions from preceding research may not be applicable to tomorrow's common online context. Thus, possible future developments in the online environment should be considered when projecting the validity of behavioural findings forward.

[handwritten margin notes: *online env is constantly evolving so too should research* *be continually updated*]

References

Bossler, A. M., & Holt, T. J. (2009). On-line activities, guardianship, and malware infection: An examination of routine activities theory. *International Journal of Cyber Criminology, 3*(1), 400–420. Retrieved from www.cybercrimejournal.com/ngo2011i-jcc.pdf.

Bossler, A. M., Holt, T. J., & May, D. C. (2012). Predicting online harassment victimization among a juvenile population. *Youth & Society, 44*(4), 500–523. DOI: 10.1177/0044118X11407525.

Diener, E. (2000). Subjective well-being: The science of happiness and a proposal for a national index. *American Psychologist, 55*(1), 34–43. DOI: 10.1037/0003-066X.55.1.34.

Diener, E., & Seligman, M. E. (2004). Beyond money toward an economy of well-being. *Psychological Science in the Public Interest, 5*(1), 1–31. DOI: 10.1111/j.0963-7214.2004.00501001.x.

Dolan, P., Peasgood, T., & White, M. (2008). Do we really know what makes us happy? A review of the economic literature on the factors associated with subjective well-being. *Journal of Economic Psychology, 29*(1), 94–122. DOI: 10.1016/j.joep.2007.09.001.

Etzioni, A. (1968). Basic human needs, alienation and inauthenticity. *American Sociological Review, 33*(6), 870–885. Retrieved from http://ssrn.com/abstract=2356319.

Foxman, A., & Wolf, C. (2013). *Viral Hate: Containing Its Spread on the Internet.* New York: Palgrave Macmillan.

Grogan, S. (2007). *Body Image: Understanding Body Dissatisfaction in Men, Women and Children.* London: Routledge.

Helweg-Larsen, K., Schütt, N., & Larsen, H. B. (2012). Predictors and protective factors for adolescent Internet victimization: Results from a 2008 nationwide Danish youth survey. *Acta Paediatrica, 101*(5), 533–539. DOI: 10.1111/j.1651-2227.2011.02587.x.

Holt, T. J., Bossler, A. M., and May, D. C. (2012). Low self-control, deviant peer associations, and juvenile cyberdeviance. *American Journal of Criminal Justice, 37*(3), 378–395.

Jones, L. M., Mitchell, K. J., & Finkelhor, D. (2013). Online harassment in context: Trends from three Youth Internet Safety Surveys (2000, 2005, 2010). *Psychology of Violence, 3*(1), 53–69. DOI: 10.1037/a0030309.

Kim, E., Lee, J. A., Sung, Y., & Choi, S. M. (2016). Predicting selfie-posting behavior on social networking sites: An extension of theory of planned behavior. *Computers in Human Behavior, 62*, 116–123. DOI: 10.1016/j.chb.2016.03.078.

Kouvo, A., & Räsänen, P. (2015). Foundations of subjective well-being in turbulent times: A comparison of four European countries. *International Journal of Sociology and Social Policy, 35*(1/2), 2–17. DOI: 10.1108/IJSSP-01-2014-0005.

Lee, E., & Leets, L. (2002). Persuasive storytelling by hate groups online: Examining its effects on adolescents. *American Behavioral Scientist, 45*(6), 927–957. DOI: 10.1177/0002764202045006003.

Leets, L. (2002). Experiencing hate speech: Perceptions and responses to anti-Semitism and antigay speech. *Journal of Social Issues, 58*(2), 341–361. DOI: 10.1111/1540-4560.00264.

Leets, L., & Giles, H. (1997). Words as weapons: When do they wound? Investigations of racist speech. *Human Communication Research, 24*(2), 260–301. DOI: 10.1111/j.1468-2958.1997.tb00415.x.

Livingstone, S., & Helsper, E. (2010). Balancing opportunities and risks in teenagers' use of the Internet: The role of online skills and Internet self-efficacy. *New Media & Society, 12*(2), 309–329. DOI: 10.1177/1461444809342697.

Minkkinen, J., Oksanen, A., Näsi, M., Keipi, T., Kaakinen, M., Keipi, T., & Räsänen, P. (2016). Does social belonging to primary groups protect young people from the effects of pro-suicide sites? A comparative study of four countries. *Crisis: The Journal of Crisis Intervention and Suicide Prevention, 37*(1), 31–41. DOI: 10.1027/0227-5910/a000356.

Mitchell, K. J., Finkelhor, D., Wolak, J., Ybarra, M. L., & Turner, H. (2011). Youth Internet victimization in a broader victimization context. *Journal of Adolescent Health, 48*(2), 128–134. DOI: 10.1016/j.jadohealth.2010.06.009.

Noll, J. G., Shenk, C. E., Barnes, J. E., & Haralson, K. J. (2013). Association of maltreatment with high-risk Internet behaviors and offline encounters. *Pediatrics, 131*(2), 510–517. DOI: 10.1542/peds.2012-1281.

Näsi, M., Räsänen, P., Hawdon, J., Holkeri, E., & Oksanen, A. (2015). Exposure to online hate material and social trust among Finnish youth. *Information Technology & People, 28*(3), 607–622. DOI: 10.1108/ITP-09-2014-0198.

Näsi, M., Räsänen, P., Oksanen, A., Hawdon, J., Keipi, T., & Holkeri, E. (2014). Association between online harassment and exposure to harmful online content: A cross-national comparison between the United States and Finland. *Computers in Human Behavior, 41*(December), 137–145. DOI: 10.1016/j.chb.2014.09.019.

Oksanen, A., & Keipi, T. (2013). Young people as victims of crime on the Internet: A population-based study in Finland. *Vulnerable Children & Youth Studies, 8*(4), 298–309. DOI: 10.1080/17450128.2012.752119.

Oksanen, A., Hawdon, J., Holkeri, E., Näsi, M., & Räsänen, P. (2014). Exposure to online hate among young social media users. *Sociological Studies of Children & Youth, 18*, 253–273. DOI: 10.1108/S1537-466120140000018021.

Proctor, C. L., Linley, P. A., & Maltby, J. (2009). Youth life satisfaction: A review of the literature. *Journal of Happiness Studies, 10*(5), 583–630. DOI: 10.1007/s10902-008-9110-9.

Robins, R. W., Hendin, H. M., & Trzesniewski, K. H. (2001). Measuring global self-esteem: Construct validation of a single-item measure and the Rosenberg Self-Esteem Scale. *Personality and Social Psychology Bulletin, 27*(2), 151–161. DOI: 10.1177/0146167201272002.

Räsänen, P. (2008). The aftermath of the ICT revolution? Media and communication technology preferences in Finland in 1999 and 2004. *New Media & Society, 10*(2), 225–245. DOI: 10.1177/1461444807086471.

Räsänen, P., Hawdon, J., Holkeri, E., Näsi, M., Keipi, T., & Oksanen, A. (2016). Targets of online hate: Examining determinants of victimization among young Finnish Facebook users. *Violence & Victims, 31*(4). DOI: 10.1891/0886-6708.VV-D-14-00079.

Sarpila, O. (2014). Attitudes towards performing and developing erotic capital in consumer culture. *European Sociological Review, 30*(3), 302–313. DOI: 10.1093/esr/jct037.

Schuessler, K. F., & Fisher, G. A. (1985). Quality of life research and sociology. *Annual Review of Sociology, 11*, 129–149. DOI: 10.1146/annurev.so.11.080185.001021.

Sourander, A., Brunstein Klomek, A., Ikonen, M., Lindroos, J., Luntamo, T., Koskelainen, M., et al. (2010). Psychological risk factors associated with cyberbullying among adolescents. A population-based study. *Archives of General Psychiatry, 67*(7), 720–728. DOI: 10.1001/archgenpsychiatry.2010.79.

Tokunaga, R. S. (2010). Following you home from school: A critical review and synthesis of research on cyberbullying victimization. *Computers in Human Behavior, 26*(3), 277–287. DOI: 10.1016/j.chb.2009.11.014.

Tynes, B. (2006). Children, adolescents, and the culture of online hate. In N. E. Dowd, D. G. Singer & R. F. Wilson (Eds.), *Handbook of Children, Culture, and Violence* (pp. 267–289). Thousand Oaks, CA: Sage.

Veenhoven, R. (2010). Greater happiness for a greater number: Is that possible and desirable? *Journal of Happiness Studies, 11*(5), 605–629. DOI: 10.1007/s10902-010-9204-z.

Veenhoven, R. (2012). Happiness: Also known as "life satisfaction" and "subjective well-being". In K. C. Land, A. C. Michalos & M. J. Sirgy (Eds.), *Handbook of Social Indicators and Quality of Life Research* (pp. 63–77). Dordrecht: Springer. DOI: 10.1007/978-94-007-2421-1.

Waldron, J. (2012). *The Harm in the Hate Speech.* Cambridge, MA: Harvard University Press.

Whittle, H., Hamilton-Giachritsis, C., Beech, A., & Collings, G. (2013). A review of young people's vulnerabilities to online grooming. *Aggression and Violent Behavior, 18*(1), 135–146. DOI: 10.1016/j.avb.2012.11.008.

6   Harm-advocating content online

6.1 Extreme becoming mainstream

On 11 May 2016 a young French woman broadcast her suicide on the Periscope live video-streaming service. The live footage was reportedly seen by a number of users and it was quickly erased by Twitter, the company that owns Periscope. This incident is an extreme example of how online and offline realities have merged. The Periscope suicide was not the first online suicide, however. One of the most famous of these cases involved a Swedish man who committed suicide online during a webcam feed in 2010. The man had stated his intention of hanging himself, which at first led many people to comment with empathy. Others did not believe him and called him a "troll" and an "attention whore". The video, which is still online, shows the man hanging himself, slowly losing breath and finally dying. There are a number of other cases where viewers or online commentators have encouraged and motivated individuals to commit various horrible acts.

Besides online suicide footage, the 2000s have seen a rise in various extreme and pathological communities that share information about ways to deliberately harm oneself. This self-directed hate expands the variety of harmful material already discussed in this book. Unfortunately, the Internet facilitates a myriad of communities devoted to self-hatred, harm and suicide. Some of them share material on death, murder and suicide on a wide scale while encouraging and instructing others to commit similar destructive actions. This material is created and distributed within small communities and is readily accessible to those seeking such exposure. We refer to such communities as harm-advocating online communities.

Exposure to harm-advocating content is not a particularly new issue. In a wider research context, violent games and movies have long been the subject of debate, particularly in terms of their implications for young people (Anderson et al., 2010; Bushman & Anderson, 2001; Ferguson & Kilburn, 2009). However, with the Internet, there is now an abundance of potentially harmful and hateful material online, including increasing amounts of what can be described as disturbing content. Given the various platforms available for online sharing, such material is often user-generated and distributed within small communities. This is very different from the role of violent media in past decades. It has been argued that both the enhanced accessibility of various media online and the scale of young people's Internet use point to the potential for new forms of risks (Jones, Mitchell & Finkelhor, 2011; Livingstone, Haddon, Görzig & Ólafsson, 2011).

Livingstone and Smith (2014) note that significant gaps in the research remain. These gaps are largely a result of the rapid changes in the technological environment. Different forms of online risks remain a relatively new research topic and so there is a need for more empirical research regarding the different associations of online risks with wellbeing. In this chapter we will first review some of the most common harm-advocating online sites and communities. We will then show empirical results regarding the exposure of adolescents and young adults in the US, the UK, Germany and Finland to such material, and how such exposure is related to their wellbeing.

6.2 The scope of harm-advocating online content

Harm-advocating online content is by definition unhealthy due to its promotion of ideas that are both physically and psychologically harmful, as determined by the mainstream of scientific knowledge. Past research has distinguished between risk and harm, risk representing a probability of harm and harm being defined as experienced damage (Breakwell, 2010; Schoon, 2006). Exposure to online content, along with offline factors, can have an effect on the wellbeing of young people through both the likelihood of facing risk, and the possibility of that risk being considered harmful (Livingstone & Görzig, 2014).

The notions of risk and actual harm often go hand in hand. Pre-existing psychological and social difficulties offline may lead to risk-taking online and eventually to actual harm to wellbeing (Noll, Shenk, Barnes & Haralson, 2013). In the online setting, it is common for users to be drawn to others with whom they are able to identify (Oksanen, Hawdon & Räsänen, 2014). A young person with mental health problems may find a sense of validation or community through contact with others having similar problems. From the point of view of this chapter and related research, harm-advocating online communities are analogical to online hate groups. Both might be attractive for some young people and eventually induce an identification with negative things, for example a life fixated on death, suicide ideation or self-harm.

We focus here on four common forms of harm-advocating content, namely sites and communities promoting self-injury, suicide and eating disorders and portrayals of death and dying. All of these have fundamental links to online hate in more general terms. Pro-self-harm and pro-suicide communities intentionally support self-hatred, which is not uncommon for pro-eating disorder communities as well. Death sites portray extremely graphic images and videos of real murders, fatal accidents and visible violence to people which could be considered as an act of hatred itself.

Pro-self-injury content

Non-suicidal self-injury (NSSI) involves the mutilation of one's bodily tissue without suicidal intent and is a common phenomenon among young people (Favazza, 1998; Nock, 2010; Skegg, 2005). Self-mutilation and cutting are often cherished and even glorified in popular culture and are quite usual. Self-mutilation has been used in performance art and popular music for its shock effect, although the actual shock has worn off during the past decades. According to Armando Favazza (1996), self-mutilation is a cross-cultural phenomenon that may take a variety of forms, from skin cutting and burning to finger amputation and testicle crushing. Despite the extreme nature of some forms of body mutilation, most are non-suicidal. It is a coping method for those who might otherwise take much more severe action.

The rise of pro-self-injury content online coincides with the rise of social networking. Whitlock, Powers and Eckenrode (2006) studied users of self-injury message boards and found that most of the users were females aged 12 to 20. Lewis and colleagues (2011) carried out a study where they examined hundreds of NSSI videos found on YouTube. Their analysis showed that the content was graphic and the videos were rated favourably by their viewers. The authors argue that the existence of such material in mainstream social media such as YouTube may in fact foster the normalisation of self-injury. According to the EU Kids Online findings, 7 per cent of 11–16-year-olds had visited user-generated sites on ways of physically harming or hurting oneself during the past twelve months (Livingstone et al., 2011, p. 98).

> This is a pro-self harm community mainly for cutters. We may glorify, honor, and admire cutting or any other form of self-harm in our entries. Do not and I repeat DO NOT be critical towards our members. If you do not like what we do then leave. It is as simple as that. We do not need to hear your rude remarks and as soon as you leave a comment that will upset the community then you will be banned from the community.
>
> Please post any pictures behind a lj-cut. No teasers. Images and posts may be triggering … so enter at your own risk. If you think you can quit cutting … then good for you … but we don't want to hear about it so just leave … just remember, we will always be here for when you slip up, because you WILL slip up. believe me.
>
> (icut Diary from LiveJournal social networking site; http://icut.livejournal.com/profile)

Pro-suicide content

Pro-suicide content is an even more severe form of self-hatred found online. This involves sites and communities that both encourage people to commit suicide and enable users to share their suicidal ideas, death fantasies and intentions, including concrete advice on how to carry out lethal acts (Becker & Schmidt, 2004; Biddle, Donovan, Hawton, Kapur & Gunnell, 2008; Kemp &

Collings, 2011; Minkkinen et al., 2016a; Recupero, Harms & Noble, 2008). People may also form a pact involving their wish to end their lives. Online pro-suicide content raised much discussion during the 2000s (Biddle et al., 2008; Luxton, June & Fairall, 2012; Rajagopal, 2004). The phenomenon first became known in Asian countries, especially Japan, where the Internet was linked to suicide pacts. These early 2000s cases involved people who knew each other beforehand and who committed suicide together (Harris, 2015; Rajagobal, 2004).

One of the most well-known examples of pro-suicide communities is ASH (alt.suicide.holiday), a discussion group in the Usenet platform during the early 1990s, before the commercial Internet era. The ASH community started off by reporting suicide news during holidays; users soon began sharing their own suicidal ideas and developed their own language around suicide (Niezen, 2013). The social media era has greatly facilitated the sharing of a variety of material that promotes and glorifies suicide. The Suicidal Children blog on Tumblr (http://suicide-children.tumblr.com/), for example, posts suicide notes and people jumping under a train in a very graphic manner. Even in terms of extreme topics, the social media era has made finding other like-minded people throughout the world far easier, all accessible within a few clicks.

According to an EU Kids Online survey 5 per cent of children aged 11–16 had seen sites on ways of committing suicide online (Livingstone, Haddon, Görzig & Ólafsson, 2011). Dunlop and colleagues' (2011) survey of young Americans aged 14 to 24 reveals that 59 per cent had drawn information about suicide from online sources. Yet there is a lack of cross-national studies concerning the characteristics of adolescents and young adults who are perhaps the most sizeable audience of harm-advocating online content, due to the high prevalence of self-harming behaviour and eating disorders among this age group (see Hawton, Saunders & O'Connor, 2012).

It is important to underline that most online content on suicide does not in fact advocate it. The Internet is also home to various self-help and support groups that aim to provide positive feedback and encourage wellbeing for their members (Barak, Boniel-Nissim & Suler, 2008; Obst & Stafurik, 2010; Tanis, 2007). A study based on web search engines by Recupero and colleagues (2008) found that only 11 per cent of suicide web hits were actually pro-suicide. Kemp and Collings (2011) assessed the visibility of such material using a web crawling data collection strategy. They found that pro-suicide sites tend to be a marginal phenomenon compared to sites dedicated to suicide prevention.

> This site was designed to help people thinking of killing themselves. That help might consist of informing of the dangers of particular methods. And there are many dangers, in many methods. They aren't on this site to dishearten you, or overwhelm you with information, it is just the facts. A successful, painless suicide takes a lot of research and preparation. And, if you read as much information as I have, you will realise it does take effort.
>
> (Lost All Hope site, http://lostallhope.com/)

Some sites also attempt to carefully instruct suicidal web surfers to continue their lives. Lost All Hope (http://lostallhope.com/) considers itself "one of the most comprehensive suicide resources on the web". It lists suicide methods by lethality, time of dying and agony produced and it also gives further academic material on the topic. The style of Lost All Hope is fact-oriented. It encourages people to seek help if necessary and gives details about why people should not kill themselves on impulse. It also directs people to potential social support, including help lines. In other words, despite the site being oriented to preparing people to kill themselves, it simultaneously emphasises a view that suicide is a definitive and final solution that cannot be reversed and must therefore be well thought through.

A review of fourteen empirical studies by Daine and colleagues (2013) showed that the Internet can have both a positive and a negative influence on young people at risk of self-harm or suicide. For example, users of suicide bulletin board systems have reported either anti- or pro-suicide goals, namely towards recovery from suicidal feelings or for help in preparation for suicide (Sueki & Eichenberg, 2012). Dunlop and colleagues (2011) demonstrated that exposure to suicide stories in online discussion forums was associated with increased suicidal ideation. Longitudinal studies by Sueki reported similar findings, indicating that suicide-related Internet use (e.g. accessing information about suicide methods) increased suicidal ideation and depression (Sueki, 2013; Sueki, Yonemoto, Takeshima & Inagaki, 2014).

Pro-eating disorder content

Over the last decade, the emergence of pro-eating disorder content has become a growing public health concern. With the help of information technologies, such communities are easily accessible and interactive, encouraging harmful weight loss and weight control practices (Custers, 2015; Juarascio, Shoaib & Timko, 2010; Lewis & Arbuthnott, 2012; Oksanen et al., 2015; Oksanen, Garcia & Räsänen, 2016; Rodgers, Lowy, Halperin & Franko, 2016). Although bulimia is more common than anorexia (Abraham, 2016), the majority of online content focuses on pro-anorexia (Lewis & Arbuthnott, 2012). Both pro-anorexia (i.e. pro-ana) and pro-bulimia (i.e. pro-mia) content includes advice on how to lose weight through interactive discussion forums and promotes "thinspiration", that is, "inspirational" pictures of extremely thin bodies and personal stories about getting and keeping thin (Peebles et al., 2012).

> Hello ladies, So recently I've been doing something that really works for me and I thought I would share it with you. Every time I'm about to binge or break a fast, I read one of these pictures i have saved on my phone. I thought it wouldn't work but after reading these messages on these pictures, I really feel less hungry and less like eating. I'll share them in this post and maybe they'll help some of you.
> ("How I Stop Myself From Eating" post to the Pro-Ana Lifestyle site, https://theproanalifestyleforever.wordpress.com/)

Pro-eating disorder sites and communities offer a platform for open and anonymous discussion of issues related to eating disorders, for gaining knowledge and support about losing weight, and for receiving social and emotional support through a sense of belonging or simply being listened to (Custers, 2015; Oksanen et al., 2016; Rodgers, Skowron & Chabrol, 2012). Pro-eating disorder communities often advocate thinness as a lifestyle choice rather than treatment as a mental disorder (Borzekowski, Schenk, Wilson & Peebles, 2010; Conrad & Rondini, 2010; Harper, Sperry & Thompson, 2008), but the material is not homogenous and user stances towards eating disorders do differ (Brotsky & Giles, 2007; Csipke & Horne, 2007; Strife & Rickard, 2011). Content analysis of pro-eating disorder sites shows that users express much mutual support and solidarity in their comments (Borzekowski et al., 2010). Hence, members are likely to identify strongly with these communities, making it difficult for parents or professionals to intervene.

Pro-eating disorder communities are found on various social media sites, including Facebook (Teufel et al., 2013), YouTube (Oksanen et al., 2015; Syed-Abdul et al., 2013), Twitter (Arseniev-Koehler, Lee, McCormick & Moreno, 2016), Instagram, Pinterest (Custers, 2015), and Flickr (Yom-Tov, Fernandez-Luque, Weber & Crain, 2012). The EU Kids Online report found that 10 per cent of 11–16-year-olds had seen pro-eating disorder content. Exposure was particularly high among 14–16-year-old girls (19 per cent) (Livingstone et al., 2011, p. 98). According to Custers and Van den Bulck (2009), almost 13 per cent of girls and nearly 6 per cent of boys aged 13, 15 and 17 had visited pro-anorexia websites. According to the study, girls who visited such sites had a higher drive for thinness and perfectionism as well as a more negative perception of their appearance. Similarly, members of pro-ana communities have been found to report high levels of disordered eating (Harper, Sperry & Thompson, 2008; Rodgers et al., 2012).

Real death content

Another pathological online genre is death video sites dedicated to portraying actual murders. In the history of Western popular culture, there is an entire mythology constructed around the portrayal of human death. The term "snuff film" was coined by Ed Sanders in relation to the Charles Manson family murders and their alleged plans to film the killings. *Snuff* was the title of a 1976 splatter horror film which stirred up a great deal of controversy in the US at the time (Stine, 1999). "Snuff" means supposed real footage of death.

Although most people in the Western world are used to seeing violence in movies and television series and even on televised news reports, there is a peculiar interest in both violent and accidental deaths of real people, as well as torture, maiming and abuse. Earlier, videos of these might have circulated as illegal VHS-tapes, but the Internet has provided a whole new platform for gore and shock sites, and some of the content can even be found through mainstream video-sharing sites. Some of the earliest of these sites, such as Rotten.com, were started as early as the mid-1990s.

An analysis by Slater (2005) of 166 websites portraying extreme violence showed that almost half of them originated in the US (45 per cent), followed by the UK (12 per cent). Only 3 per cent of such sites were from Germany and an even smaller proportion from other countries. The sites typically included videos and images and provided links to other sites. These sites show a variety of forms of violence: they may represent violence as humorous, include directly hateful violence, animal violence, sexual violence, combat violence and very gory scenes of violence in general. More recently, social media have made it even easier to share content with others who share similar interests.

Best Gore website contains gory images and videos and depictions of (but not limited to):

- death, including beheadings, executions, suicides, murders, electrocution, stoning, torching, drowning
- accidents, including car crashes, motorcycle crashes, workplace accidents, sexual accidents, animal attacks
- war, including bomb victims often involving children, white phosphorus attacks, decapitation of POVs, mass executions, biological warfare, genocide, ethnic cleansing, torture
- diseases, including poisoning, heart attacks, terminal illness patients, drug abuse
- unusual fetishes, including needle fetishes, blood fetishes, genital mutilation
- body modifications, including self mutilation and more

(Best Gore: Welcome to Best Gore introduction text,
www.bestgore.com/)

Luka Magnotta is a recent peculiar representative of this genre. Magnotta, who had a career as a pornographic actor, killed a Chinese exchange student, dismembered her and ate parts of her, and then mailed the remaining limbs to elementary school and political party offices in Canada. Videos of his actions were posted to Bestgore.com directly after the crime. Magnotta is just one among others in the Western world who has been fascinated with the possibilities offered by the Internet. In addition to live online footage of suicides, it is unfortunately obvious that many are fascinated by the potential shock value offered by live murder. A recent demonstration of online hatred has been the actions taken by the ISIS terrorist group whose members have posted beheading videos on mainstream social media sites such as YouTube beginning in July 2014.

A survey of American youth reported that only 4 per cent of young people aged 10 to 15 had seen death sites (Ybarra, Mitchell & Korchmaros, 2011). Viewing such sites was associated with seriously violent behaviour in a nationally representative US study (Ybarra et al., 2008). However, it is important to keep in mind that media violence might influence a small minority of highly aggressive subjects who are likely to seek out violent content (Baumeister, 1997, pp. 278–280). According to a study by Michael D. Slater (2003), alienation from school and family was predictive of browsing of violent online sites. Eventually, such exposure may have had negative impacts on wellbeing, as is proposed by the downward spiral model by Slater (2003) and colleagues.

6.3 Harm-advocating content from a cross-national perspective

Ellen Helsper and her colleagues (2013) created a cross-national categorisation of young Internet users tracking the likelihood of them encountering different online risks. It found that Nordic countries and the Netherlands belong to a category of "supported risky explorers": these are experienced social media users with strong parental support who also encounter more risks online, including harm-advocating material. On the other hand, children in the UK, Germany and most middle and southern European countries were found to be much more protected due to, for example, more restrictions on usage put in place by parents. Language barriers can also serve as a protective factor among young children.

However, despite such categorisation of cross-cultural differences in potential risk exposure, a study by Sueki and Eichenberg (2012) found no country difference between American and Japanese suicide bulletin board users. Furthermore, Keipi and his colleagues (2015) compared the US and Finland and found that exposure rates to pro-suicide, pro-self-harm, pro-eating disorder and death sites were remarkably similar in the two countries. They concluded that cultural differences may not always significantly predict online behaviour. Thus users may be exposed to similar content due to the globalising effects of the Internet despite differences between societies. Here, we turn to these differences and similarities between populations in more detail.

Our data included general risk measures on exposure to harm-advocating content. The items were based on previous studies by research groups in both Europe (Livingstone et al., 2011) and the US (Ybarra et al., 2011). A set of four questions was used to measure exposure to harm-advocating websites and online communities. The respondents were asked whether they had seen the following in the past twelve months (yes/no answer option): (1) "sites about ways of physically harming or hurting yourself" (pro-self-injury content), (2) "sites about ways of committing suicide" (pro-suicide content), (3) "sites about ways to be very thin (e.g. sites relating to eating disorders)" (pro-eating disorder content) and (4) "sites dedicated to showing the deaths or murders of real people" (death content). These four items were used as dependent variables and operationalised as advocating harm to online users (e.g. pro-eating disorder, Livingstone et al., 2011; pro-suicide and pro-self-injury, Minkkinen, Oksanen, Kaakinen, Keipi & Räsänen, 2016b), as they address particular methods of harming oneself. Previous studies show that instructions on self-harm are part of pro-anorexia and pro-suicide sites and communities (Biddle et al., 2008; Boero & Pascoe, 2012; Borzekowski et al., 2010), and thus provide a clear risk for young people who become exposed to such content.

Figure 6.1 shows the proportions of 15–30-year-olds who had seen harm-advocating online material in the US, the UK, Germany and Finland. As the

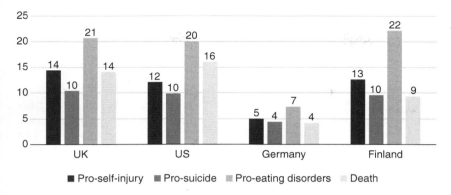

Figure 6.1 Exposure to harm-advocating online content among 15–30-year-old respondents in the UK, the US, Germany and Finland. Percentages.

figure indicates, potentially disturbing online content was generally seen by fewer people than online hate content. Pro-eating disorder content (17 per cent) was the most common form of material seen by young people in the UK, the US, Germany and Finland, followed by pro-self-injury (11 per cent) and death sites (11 per cent). Of all our respondents, only 8 per cent had seen pro-suicide material. Yet we have to put these figures into perspective. The figures could be considered high due to the extreme nature of some of the material. In fact, in the US, 31 per cent had visited at least some site involving harm-advocating content during the past twelve months. The corresponding figures were 29 per cent for the UK, 28 per cent for Finland and 12 per cent for Germany.

Consistent with our findings in previous chapters, German respondents were significantly less likely to witness harm-advocating online content than youth in the other three countries ($p < 0.001$), while the differences between Finland, the UK and the US were small. Furthermore, only 5 per cent of Germans reported visiting sites about how to physically harm or hurt oneself, while the percentages were higher in the UK (14 per cent), Finland (13 per cent) and the US (12 per cent). A similar division was evident with suicide sites, as less than 5 per cent of Germans had visited such sites, whereas approximately 10 per cent of respondents in other countries reported doing so. Again, approximately 7 per cent of the German respondents had visited sites dedicated to being very thin, compared with over 20 per cent for the three other countries. Finally, just over 4 per cent of the German respondents had visited sites dedicated to showing actual deaths and murders during the last year, whereas the figure for Finland was nearly 10 per cent, for the UK 14 per cent, and for the US 16 per cent.

There are a number of potential explanation for these differences by country, some of which have already been discussed in Chapters 4 and 5. First of all, previous studies have shown that harm-advocating material is primarily on English-language sites originating in the US and also in the UK. This might

Theo US highest exposure

explain why US respondents have the highest rates of exposure to death sites. Second, we know from other studies that parents in some countries are more protective when it comes to their children's Internet usage (Helsper et al., 2013). Although our sample is not restricted to children, such protective attitudes towards online content might continue during late adolescence and emerging adulthood. Third, language might play a role (see Chapter 5 above). This might explain why the percentages among young Finns were often similar to those in the UK and the US. As there is only a limited amount of content in Finnish, Finns seek out English-language content. The fourth explanation has to do with the average mental health of young people. German young people aged 15 to 29 have, for example, relatively low suicide rates compared to Finnish and US rates (WHO, 2014; see also Hawton et al., 2012). This might partially explain the results, especially as we are discussing a relatively pathological online phenomenon.

6.4 Harm-advocating content and its associations with wellbeing

Similar to what has already been seen in the previous chapters of this book, exposure to harm-advocating online content is likely to vary by individuals' socio-demographic background and various behavioural characteristics. In the following, Figures 6.2–6.5 show proportions of exposure to pro-self-injury, pro-suicide, pro-eating disorder and death content by gender, age, living with parents, immigrant background, frequency of Internet use and exposure to and victimisation by online hate.

First, Figure 6.2 shows that males were more likely to encounter pro-self-injury contents than females (*p*<0.05). This is somewhat surprising, given past research findings which show that intentional self-harm is more common among

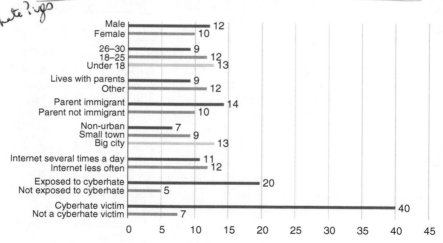

Figure 6.2 Exposure to pro-self-injury content by respondents' background characteristics. Percentages.

[handwritten: Men enjoy seeing others so victims? → interpret for us or let us do it]

[handwritten right margin: males see more self injury stuff but females do it more]

young females than young males, though the gender difference has been found to decrease with age (Hawton et al., 2012; Skegg, 2005; see also Whitlock et al., 2006). Younger respondents were slightly more likely to see pro-self-injury sites. Our results show some evidence of the guardianship factor (see Chapter 3 above for RAT theory), as those living at home were less likely to visit pro-self-injury sites ($p<0.05$) than those not living at home. Immigrant background, on the other hand, increased the likelihood of exposure to pro-self-injury content ($p<0.001$) as respondents with an immigrant parent were more likely to see such material than those who did not have an immigrant parent. There are no major differences in terms of frequency of daily Internet use, but those who had either seen online hate or been victimised by it were significantly more likely to visit pro-self-injury sites.

[handwritten right margin: males more pro suicide]

Figure 6.3 shows that males were more likely to encounter pro-suicide ($p<0.05$) content than females. This is not surprising since suicide rates are much higher among males aged 15 to 29 than females of the same age (Hawton et al., 2012; Skegg, 2005; WHO, 2014). As regards the potential guardianship factor, those respondents who were still living at home were less likely to visit pro-suicide sites ($p<0.01$) than those who were not living at home. However, immigrant background also increased the likelihood of exposure to pro-suicide content ($p<0.01$) as respondents with immigrant parents were more likely to see such material than those who did not have immigrant parents. Differences in terms of frequency of daily online use were minor, but both exposure and victimisation to online hate were strongly associated with visiting pro-suicide sites.

[handwritten right margin: females pro-ana]

Figure 6.4 shows that females were more likely to visit pro-eating disorders sites ($p<0.001$) than males. These findings are unsurprising, as we know that eating disorders are more common among the female population (e.g. Fairburn & Harrison, 2003; Treasure, Claudino & Zucker, 2010). It also appears that the oldest respondents are the least exposed to pro-eating disorder content exposure

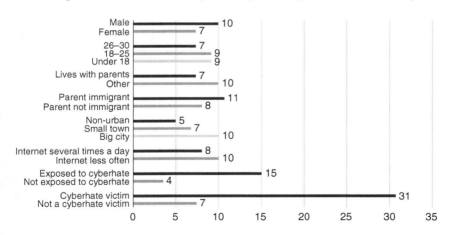

Figure 6.3 Exposure to pro-suicide content by respondents' background characteristics. Percentages.

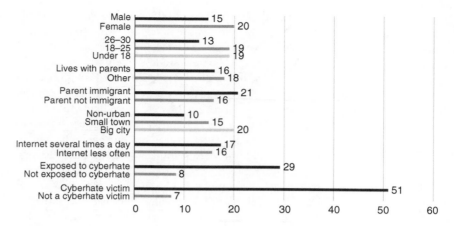

Figure 6.4 Exposure to pro-eating disorders content by respondents' background characteristics. Percentages.

($p<0.001$). Differences between those living at home with their parents and others were not significant. Furthermore, immigrant background was associated with visiting pro-eating disorder sites ($p<0.01$), respondents with immigrant parents being more likely to see such material than those who did not have immigrant parents. There were only minor differences between those who used the Internet several times a day and those who did so less often. Victims of cyberhate were far more likely to visit pro-eating disorder sites (51 per cent vs 7 per cent, $p<0.001$). Also, exposure to online hate was strongly associated with seeing pro-eating disorder content. These figures are very high compared to those who had not been exposed to cyberhate or been victimised by it.

Figure 6.5 shows that males were more likely to encounter death content than females ($p<0.001$). This finding is supported by earlier studies, which have also shown that males visit death sites more often than females (Ybarra et al., 2008, 2011). Age and living with parents were not significant background factors for seeing death sites. Those with an immigrant background were more likely to see pro-eating disorder content ($p<0.001$) than those who did not have immigrant parents. Frequency of daily Internet use was not associated with visiting death sites. Those exposed to cyberhate and those victimised by it were strongly associated with seeing death sites.

Overall, Figures 6.2–6.5 show that age differences appear not to be very significant, but the youngest respondents were generally more likely to see harm-advocating online content. From a developmental perspective this is understandable, as young people face rapid changes in their life events especially during emerging adulthood but also during late adolescence. This can lead to increased instability and incidences of psychopathology (Arnett, 2000; Schulenberg & Zarrett, 2006). Thus, it is at this age and life phase that danger from exposure to harm-advocating content online is at its highest.

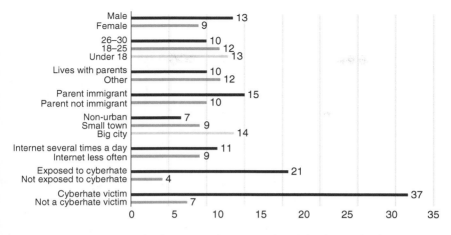

Figure 6.5 Exposure to death content by respondents' background characteristics. Percentages.

We did not find statistically significant differences between those who reported using the Internet several times a day and those who use it more seldom. Yet users accessing harm-advocating sites reported using more ICT and social media services than those who did not ($p<0.001$). Hence, it seems that those visiting harm-advocating sites tend to be more active users at least in terms of the range of different sites and services used (Keipi et al., 2015). This finding is generally in line with results presented in Chapters 4 and 5 above where we show how ICT activity is associated with online hate exposure and online victimisation.

One of our more striking findings is, however, that both exposure to and victimisation by online hate are very strongly associated with seeing harm-advocating online material. Visiting pro-self-injury, pro-suicide, pro-eating disorder and death sites is much more common among those who have also seen hateful or degrading writings or speech online that inappropriately attack certain groups of people or individuals. To a certain extent, this may be an expected finding due to overlap between these types of material online. Death sites, for example, could be considered hate sites. However, we also find very high figures among online hate victims. There is a notable difference here compared to those who have not had experience of personal victimisation ($p<0.001$). For example, 40 per cent of cyberhate victims had visited pro-self-injury sites, compared to 7 per cent of those who were not victims.

In Figure 6.6 we provide associations between exposure to harm-advocating online content and subjective wellbeing (SWB), similar to those provided in Chapter 5 on online victimisation. Our measures of SWB include happiness, satisfaction in terms of economic condition, trust of other people and self-esteem. Here, we examine how exposure to harm-advocating online content is associated with

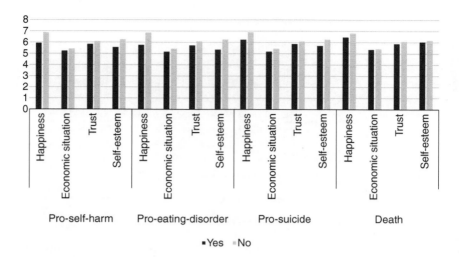

Figure 6.6 Exposure to harm-advocating online content and its association with well-being. Means (evaluated on a scale from 1 to 10).

these. As we can see from the results, those who had visited harm advocating sites generally reported lower SWB on all of the measured degrees. Differences in exposed and unexposed groups were strong in terms of perceived happiness ($p<0.001$). Users who had visited pro-self-injury, pro-suicide and pro-eating disorder sites also reported lower self-esteem consistently ($p<0.001$). Those who had visited pro-suicide sites reported not only lower happiness ($p<0.001$) and self-esteem ($p<0.001$), but also lower economic satisfaction and trust.

6.5 The downward spiral of negative online behaviour

Our data show that many young people had visited harm-advocating sites online. Figures for seeing at least one type of harm-advocating online content were relatively high, especially in the US (31 per cent), the UK (29 per cent) and Finland (28 per cent), but significantly lower in Germany (12 per cent). This difference between countries, which cannot be entirely explained by our data, is linked to various factors that potentially protect German youth from witnessing extreme online content. The same findings also underline that young Finnish online users are in fact a very close match to those from the US and UK.

We were also able to show consistent background factors of exposure to harm-advocating sites. Not only are the youngest respondents the most vulnerable group, they become even more so when they have moved away from the family home. Since current online behaviour is grounded in social interaction, such material may carry different implications for adolescents and young adults compared to traditional media exposure. As already noted in previous chapters, online risks are sometimes linked to potential problems faced in offline

You get away from bone most vulnerable

circumstances, and we should be especially concerned about those young people who lack the proper contacts in their offline lives. Some problems may be pre-existing, only to grow stronger eventually in the online setting.

Although some young users have life-affirming goals when searching for harm-advocating material (Daine et al., 2013; Sueki & Eichenberg, 2012), the general impacts of accessing harm-advocating online material are negative (Sueki et al., 2014). We see this in our findings as well, though we have to bear in mind that our data are cross-sectional. Those who had visited harm-advocating sites reported consistently lower subjective wellbeing. It is therefore important to recognise the existence of harm-advocating and extreme online communities and the relative ease with which young people may encounter this material and the communities producing it.

Online hate is a phenomenon tied closely to harm-advocating sites and communities. Sometimes the link is very direct, as death content is very often hate content. This connection has become obvious, for instance in the case of hate propaganda by ISIS which has disseminated it to mainstream social media since 2013. However, self-directed sites such as pro-self-injury and pro-suicide sites have links with online hate phenomena as well. In our data, these links are quite obvious, especially when analysing online hate victims, as 65 per cent of the online hate victims had visited harm-advocating websites.

Slater and colleagues (2003) have demonstrated how exposure to very disturbing online content can be conceptualised as a downward spiral. In other words, existing psychological problems may motivate some individuals to seek potentially harmful online material. Thus exposure to this material can further magnify the problems. Harm-advocating sites such as pro-suicide sites may also contribute to a form of tunnel vision where participants actively attempt to block out options to solve their problems (Harris, 2015). The downward spiral has been demonstrated in school shooter cases, where the perpetrator was originally faced with problems in the online context only to become fixated with revenge on others. However, aggressors have often been unable to find support for their plans in the offline setting, and this drives them to become tremendously active online in order to search for validation there (Oksanen, Nurmi, Vuori & Räsänen, 2013; Oksanen et al., 2014; Sandberg, Oksanen, Berntzen & Kiilakoski, 2014).

Harm-advocating online material is user-generated, easily accessible and seen by many young people. Since current online behaviour is grounded in social interaction, such material may carry different implications for young people compared to traditional media. It is therefore important to recognise the potential implications of harm-advocating and extreme online communities and the relative ease with which young people may encounter this material and the communities producing it. This material can, and does, play a role in the lives and therefore wellbeing of many. Furthermore, our main findings are also relevant to medical and healthcare practitioners working with adolescents and young adults. Professionals should be aware that when individuals with potential mental health problems go online, they are at heightened risk of encountering not only life-affirming social support but also communities that may foster anti-healthy behaviour.

References

Abraham S. (2016). *Eating Disorders: The Facts*. Oxford: Oxford University Press.

Anderson, C., Shibuya, A., Ihori, N., Swing, E. L., Bushman, B. J., Sakamoto, A., et al. (2010). Violent video game effects on aggression, empathy, and prosocial behavior in Eastern and Western countries: A meta-analytic review. *Psychological Bulletin, 136*(2), 151–173. DOI: 10.1037/a0018251.

Arnett, J. J. (2000). Emerging adulthood: A theory of development from the late teens through the twenties. *American Psychologist, 55*(5), 469–480. DOI: 10.1037//0003-066X.55.5.469.

Arseniev-Koehler, A., Lee, H., McCormick, T., & Moreno, M. A. (2016). #Proana: Pro-eating disorder socialization on Twitter. *Journal of Adolescent Health, 58*(6), 659–664. DOI: 10.1016/j.jadohealth.2016.02.012.

Barak, A., Boniel-Nissim, M., & Suler, J. (2008). Fostering empowerment in online support groups. *Computers in Human Behavior, 24*(5), 1867–1883. DOI: 10.1016/j.chb.2008.02.004.

Baumeister, R. F. (1997). *Evil: Inside Human Violence and Cruelty*. New York: W. H. Freeman.

Becker, K., & Schmidt, M. H. (2004). Internet chat rooms and suicide. *Journal of the American Academy of Child & Adolescent Psychiatry, 43*(3), 246–247. DOI: 10.1097/00004583-200403000-00002.

Biddle L., Donovan, J., Hawton, K., Kapur, N., & Gunnell, D. (2008). Public health: Suicide and the Internet. *British Medical Journal, 336*(7648), 800–802. DOI: 10.1136/bmj.39525.442674.AD.

Boero, N., & Pascoe, C. J. (2012). Pro-anorexia communities and online interaction: Bringing the pro-ana body online. *Body & Society, 18*(2), 27–57. DOI: 10.1177/1357034X12440827.

Borzekowski, D. L., Schenk, S., Wilson, J. L., & Peebles, R. (2010). e-Ana and e-Mia: A content analysis of pro-eating disorder web sites. *American Journal of Public Health, 100*(8), 1526–1534. DOI: 10.2105/AJPH.2009.172700.

Breakwell, G. M. (2010). Models of risk construction: Some applications to climate change. *Wiley Interdisciplinary Reviews: Climate Change, 1*(6), 857–870. DOI: 10.1002/wcc.74.

Brotsky, S. R., & Giles, D. (2007). Inside the "pro-ana" community: A covert online participant observation. *Eating Disorders, 15*(2), 93–109. DOI: 10.1080/10640260701190600.

Bushman, B. J., & Anderson, C. A. (2001). Media violence and the American public: Scientific facts versus media misinformation. *American Psychologist, 56*(6–7), 477–489. DOI: 10.1037//0003-066X.56.6-7.477.

Conrad, P., & Rondini, A. (2010). The Internet and medicalization: Reshaping the global body and illness. In E. Ettorre (Ed.), *Culture, Bodies and the Sociology of Health* (pp. 107–120). Farnham: Ashgate.

Csipke, E., & Horne, O. (2007). Pro-eating disorder websites: Users' opinions. *European Eating Disorders Review, 15*(3), 196–206. DOI: 10.1002/erv.789.

Custers, K. (2015). The urgent matter of online pro-eating disorder content and children: Clinical practice. *European Journal of Pediatrics, 174*(4), 429–433. DOI: 10.1007/s00431-015-2487-7.

Custers, K., & Van den Bulck, J. (2009). Viewership of pro-anorexia websites in seventh, ninth and eleventh graders. *European Eating Disorders Review, 17*(3), 214–219. DOI: 10.1002/erv.910.

Daine, K., Hawton, K., Singaravelu, V., Stewart, A., Simkin, S., & Montgomery, P. (2013). The power of the Web: A systematic review of studies of the influence of the Internet on self-harm and suicide in young people. *PloS one, 8*(10). DOI: e77555.

Dunlop, S. M., More, E., & Romer, D. (2011). Where do youth learn about suicides on the Internet, and what influence does this have on suicidal ideation? *Journal of Child Psychology and Psychiatry, 52*(10), 1073–1080. DOI: 10.1111/j.1469-7610.2011.02416.x.

Fairburn, C. G., & Harrison, P. J. (2003). Eating disorders. *The Lancet, 361*(9355), 407–416. DOI: http://dx.doi.org/10.1016/S0140-6736(03)12378-1.

Favazza, A. R. (1996). *Bodies under Siege: Self-mutilation and Body Modification in Culture and Psychiatry.* Baltimore, MD, and London: The Johns Hopkins University Press.

Favazza, A. R. (1998). The coming of age of self-mutilation. *The Journal of Nervous and Mental Disease, 186*(5), 259–268. DOI: 10.1097/00005053-199805000-00001.

Ferguson, C. J., & Kilburn, J. (2009). The public health risks of media violence: A meta-analytic review. *The Journal of Pediatrics, 154*(5), 759–763. DOI: 10.1016/j.jpeds.2008.11.033.

Harper, K., Sperry, S., & Thompson, J. K. (2008). Viewership of pro-eating disorder websites: Association with body image and eating disturbances. *International Journal of Eating Disorders, 41*(1), 92–95. DOI: 10.1002/eat.20408.

Harris, K. M. (2015). Life versus death: The suicidal mind. In E. Aboujaoude & V. Starcevic (Eds.), *Mental Health in the Digital Age: Grave Dangers, Great Promise* (pp. 135–150). New York: Oxford University Press.

Hawton, K., Saunders, K. E., & O'Connor, R. C. (2012). Self-harm and suicide in adolescents. *The Lancet, 379*(9834), 2373–2382. DOI: 10.1016/S0140-6736(12)60322-5.

Helsper, E. J., Kalmus, V., Hasebrink, W., Sagvari, B., & De Haan, J. (2013). *Country Classification: Opportunities, Risks, Harm and Parental Mediation.* London: LSE, EU Kids Online.

Jones, L., Mitchell, K., & Finkelhor, D. (2011). Trends in youth Internet victimization: Findings from three youth Internet safety surveys 2000–2010. *Journal of Adolescent Health 50*(2), 179–186. DOI: 10.1016/j.jadohealth.2011.09.015.

Juarascio, A. S., Shoaib, A., & Timko, C. A. (2010). Pro-eating disorder communities on social networking sites: A content analysis. *Eating Disorders, 18*(5), 393–407. DOI: 10.1080/10640266.2010.511918.

Keipi, T., Oksanen, A., Hawdon, J., Näsi, M., & Räsänen, P. (2015). Harm-advocating online content and subjective well-being: A cross-national study of new risks faced by youth. *Journal of Risk Research, 18*, 1–16. DOI: 10.1080/13669877.2015.1100660.

Kemp, C. G., & Collings, S. C. (2011). Hyperlinked suicide: Assessing the prominence and accessibility of suicide websites. *Crisis: The Journal of Crisis Intervention and Suicide Prevention, 32*(3), 143–151. DOI: 10.1027/0227-5910/a000068.

Lewis, S. P., & Arbuthnott, A. E. (2012). Searching for thinspiration: The nature of Internet searches for pro-eating disorder websites. *Cyberpsychology, Behavior, and Social Networking, 15*(4), 200–204. DOI: 10.1089/cyber.2011.0453.

Lewis, S. P., Heath, N. L., St Denis, J. M., & Noble, R. (2011). The scope of nonsuicidal self-injury on YouTube. *Pediatrics, 127*(3), e552–e557. DOI: 10.1542/peds.2010-2317.

Livingstone, S., & Görzig, A. (2014). When adolescents receive sexual messages on the Internet: Explaining experiences of risk and harm. *Computers in Human Behavior, 33*, 8–15. DOI: 10.1016/j.chb.2013.12.021.

Livingstone S., & Smith, P. K. (2014). Annual research review: Harms experienced by child users of online and mobile technologies: The nature, prevalence and management of sexual and aggressive risks in the digital age. *Journal of Child Psychology and Psychiatry, 55*(6), 635–654. DOI: 10.1111/jcpp. 12197.

Livingstone, S., Haddon, L., Görzig, A., & Ólafsson, K. (2011). Risks and safety on the Internet: The perspective of European children: full findings and policy implications from the EU Kids Online survey of 9–16 year olds and their parents in 25 countries. London: LSE, EU Kids Online. Retrieved from http://eprints.lse.ac.uk/33731/.

Luxton, D. D., June, J. D., & Fairall, J. M. (2012). Social media and suicide: A public health perspective. *American Journal of Public Health, 102*(2), 195–200. DOI: 10.2105/AJPH.2011.300608.

Minkkinen, J., Oksanen, A., Kaakinen, M., Keipi, T., & Räsänen P. (2016b). Victimization and exposure to pro-self-harm and pro-suicide websites: A cross-national study. *Suicide and Life-Threatening Behavior* (online first). DOI: 10.1111/sltb.12258.

Minkkinen, J., Oksanen, A., Näsi, M., Keipi, T., Kaakinen, M., Keipi, T. et al. (2016a). Does social belonging to primary groups protect young people from the effects of pro-suicide sites? A comparative study of four countries. *Crisis: The Journal of Crisis Intervention and Suicide Prevention, 37*(1), 31–41. DOI: 10.1027/0227-5910/a000356.

Niezen, R. (2013). Internet suicide: Communities of affirmation and the lethality of communication. *Transcultural Psychiatry, 50*(2), 303–322. DOI: 10.1177/13634615124 73733.

Nock, M. K. (2010). Self-injury. *Annual Review of Clinical Psychology, 6*, 339–363. DOI: 10.1146/annurev.clinpsy.121208.131258.

Noll, J. G., Shenk, C. E., Barnes, J. E., & Haralson, K. J. (2013). Association of maltreatment with high-risk Internet behaviors and offline encounters. *Pediatrics, 131*, 510–517. DOI: 10.1542/peds.2012-1281.

Obst, P., & Stafurik, J. (2010). Online we are all able bodied: Online psychological sense of community and social support found through membership of disability-specific websites promotes well-being for people living with a physical disability. *Journal of Community and Applied Social Psychology, 20*, 525–531. DOI: 10.1002/casp. 1067.

Oksanen, A., Garcia, D., & Räsänen, P. (2016). Proanorexia communities on social media. *Pediatrics, 137*(1), 1–3. DOI: 10.1542/peds.2015-3372.

Oksanen, A., Hawdon, J., & Räsänen, P. (2014) Glamorizing rampage online: School shooting fan communities on YouTube. *Technology in Society, 39*, 55–67. DOI: 10.1016/j.techsoc.2014.08.001.

Oksanen, A., Nurmi, J., Vuori, M., & Räsänen, P. (2013). Jokela: The social roots of a school shooting tragedy in Finland. In N. Böckler, T. Seeger, P. Sitzer & W. Heitmeyer (Eds.), *School Shootings: International Research, Case Studies and Concepts for Prevention* (pp. 189–215). New York: Springer. DOI: 10.1007/978-1-4614-5526-4_9.

Oksanen, A., Garcia, D., Sirola, A., Näsi, M., Kaakinen, M., Keipi, T., & Räsänen, P. (2015). Pro-anorexia and anti-pro-anorexia videos on YouTube: Sentiment analysis of user responses. *Journal of Medical Internet Research, 17*(11), e256. DOI: 10.2196/jmir.5007.

Peebles, R., Wilson, J. L., Litt, I. F., Hardy, K. K., Lock, J. D., Mann, J. R., & Borzekowski, D. L. (2012). Disordered eating in a digital age: Eating behaviors, health, and quality of life in users of websites with pro-eating disorder content. *Journal of Medical Internet Research, 14*(5), e148. DOI: 10.2196/jmir.2023.

Rajagopal, S. (2004). Suicide pacts and the Internet. *British Medical Journal,, 329*(7478), 1298–1299. DOI: 10.1136/bmj.329.7478.1298.

Recupero, P. R., Harms, S. E., & Noble, J. M. (2008). Googling suicide: Surfing for suicide information on the Internet. *Journal of Clinical Psychiatry, 69*(6), 878–888. DOI: 10.4088/JCP.v69n0601.

Rodgers, R. F., Skowron, S., & Chabrol, H. (2012). Disordered eating and group membership among members of a pro-anorexic online community. *European Eating Disorders Review, 20*(1), 9–12. DOI: 10.1002/erv.1096.

Rodgers, R. F., Lowy, A. S., Halperin, D. M., & Franko, D. L. (2016). A meta-analysis examining the influence of pro-eating disorder websites on body image and eating pathology. *European Eating Disorders Review, 24*(1), 3–8. DOI: 10.1002/erv.2390.

Sandberg, S., Oksanen, A., Berntzen, L. E., & Kiilakoski, T. (2014). Stories in action: The cultural influences of school shootings on the terrorist attacks in Norway. *Critical Studies on Terrorism, 7*(2), 277–296. DOI: 10.1080/17539153.2014.906984.

Schoon, I. (2006). *Risk and Resilience: Adaptations in Changing Times.* New York: Cambridge University Press.

Schulenberg. J. E., & Zarrett, N. R. (2006). Mental health during emerging adulthood: Continuity and discontinuity in courses, causes, and functions. In J. J. Arnett & J. L. Tanner (Eds.), *Emerging Adults in America: Coming of Age in the 21st Century* (pp. 135–172). Washington, DC: APA Books.

Skegg, K. (2005). Self-harm. *The Lancet, 366*(9495), 1471–1483. DOI: 10.1016/S0140-6736(05)67600-3.

Slater, M. D. (2003). Alienation, aggression, and sensation seeking as predictors of adolescent use of violent film, computer, and website content. *Journal of Communication, 53*(1), 105–121. DOI: 10.1111/j.1460-2466.2003.tb03008.x.

Slater, M. D., Henry, K. L., Swaim, R. C., & Anderson, L. L. (2003). Violent media content and aggressiveness in adolescents: A downward spiral model. *Communication Research, 30*(6), 713–736. DOI: 10.1177/0093650203258281.

Slater, S. (2005). The commodification of violence on the Internet: An analysis of 166 websites containing commodified violence. *Internet Journal of Criminology.* Retrieved from www.internetjournalofcriminology.com/Slater%20-%20THE%20 COMMODIFICATION%20OF%20VIOLENCE%20ON%20THE%20INTERNET. pdf.

Stine, S. A. (1999) Snuff film: The making of an urban legend. *Sceptical Inquiry, 23*(3). Retrieved from www.csicop.org/si/show/snuff_film_the_making_of_an_urban_legend/ about.

Strife, S. R., & Rickard, K. (2011). The conceptualization of anorexia: The pro-ana perspective. *Affilia, 26*(2), 213–217. DOI: 10.1177/0886109911405592.

Sueki, H. (2013). The effect of suicide-related Internet use on users' mental health: A longitudinal study. *Crisis: The Journal of Crisis Intervention and Suicide Prevention, 34*(5), 348–353. DOI: 10.1027/0227-5910/a000201.

Sueki, H., & Eichenberg, C. (2012). Suicide bulletin board systems comparison between Japan and Germany. *Death Studies, 36*(6), 565–580. DOI: 10.1080/07481187. 2011.584012.

Sueki, H., Yonemoto, N., Takeshima, T., & Inagaki, M. (2014). The impact of suicidality-related Internet use: A prospective large cohort study with young and middle-aged Internet users. *PloS one, 9*(4), e94841. DOI: 10.1371/journal.pone.0094841.

Syed-Abdul, S., Fernandez-Luque, L., Jian, W. S., Li, Y. C., Crain, S., Hsu, M. H., et al. (2013). Misleading health-related information promoted through video-based social media: Anorexia on YouTube. *Journal of Medical Internet Research, 15*(2), e30. DOI: 10.2196/jmir.2237.

Tanis, M. (2007). Online social support groups. In A. Joinson, K. McKenna, T. Postmes & U. Reips (Eds.), *The Oxford Handbook of Internet Psychology* (pp. 139–153). Oxford: Oxford University Press.

Teufel, M., Hofer, E., Junne, F., Sauer, H., Zipfel, S., & Giel, K. E. (2013). A comparative analysis of anorexia nervosa groups on Facebook. *Eating and Weight Disorders, 18*(4), 413–420. DOI: 10.1007/s40519-013-0050-y.

Treasure, J., Claudino, A. M., & Zucker, N. (2010). Eating disorders. *The Lancet, 13*(375), 583–592. DOI: 10.1016/S0140-6736(09)61748-7.

Whitlock, J. L., Powers, J. L., & Eckenrode, J. (2006). The virtual cutting edge: The Internet and adolescent self-injury. *Developmental Psychology, 42*(3), 407–417. DOI: 10.1037/0012-1649.42.3.000.

World Health Organisation (WHO) (2014) *Preventing Suicide: A Global Imperative.* Luxemburg: WHO. Retrieved from http://apps.who.int/iris/bitstream/10665/131056/1/9789241564779_eng.pdf.

Ybarra, M. L., Diener-West, M., Markow, D., Leaf, P. J., Hamburger, M., & Boxer, P. (2008). Linkages between Internet and other media violence with seriously violent behavior by youth. *Pediatrics, 122*(5), 929–937. DOI: 10.1542/peds.2007-3377.

Ybarra, M. L., Mitchell, K. J., & Korchmaros, J. D. (2011). National trends in exposure to and experiences of violence on the Internet among children. *Pediatrics, 128*(6), 1376–1386. DOI: 10.1542/peds.2011-0118.

Yom-Tov, E., Fernandez-Luque, L., Weber, I., & Crain, S. P. (2012). Pro-anorexia and pro-recovery photo sharing: A tale of two warring tribes. *Journal of Medical Internet Research, 14*(6), e151. DOI: 10.2196/jmir.2239.

7 Social spheres of online hate

7.1 The changing social milieu

London attracts millions of tourists every year. A large number of visitors flock to the main attractions that the city has to offer. Among must-see sites are Big Ben, Trafalgar Square and the famous department store Harrods; visitors then head over to hopefully catch a glimpse of the royal family in either Buckingham Palace or Kensington Palace. Now, before doing so, many visitors tend to wander into Hyde Park, a tourist destination in its own right, in order take a well-earned rest after a morning of walking. Often, depending on the time of day, weary travellers may notice a small group of people in the corner of the park, near the Marble Arch underground station. It is here that tourists come across London's famous Speakers' Corner. Throughout its vast history, extending from the 1850s, Speakers' Corner has been among the most famous venues for publicly expressing one's views.

[handwritten margin note: Speaker's Corner]

With this rich history, much like other Speakers' Corners in many other cities around the world, the public expression of an opinion or an ideology has been an important aspect of social life for a long time. Today, this phenomenon has risen to a scale never before seen. What began as a small corner beside a park or a small gathering at a coffee house has expanded exponentially. Today, various social media serve as personalised "Speakers' Corners", with the potential to reach a global audience from the convenience of one's Internet connection. This change of venue and the tools available has also meant major changes in the public, or social, sphere of opinion. The public sphere has traditionally been understood as a physical place where people gather to discuss and debate societal issues. Although places like Speakers' Corner still exist, the value and power of the venue for which it was created have diminished a great deal. Rather, it has become more of a tourist attrac-tion than a forum for facilitating actual debate. However, this does not mean that the public sphere no longer exists. Rather, it is alive and well, be it at coffee houses, bars, living rooms, street corners and anywhere people meet and socialise. The change far surpassing physical location, however, is that social media in the larger societal context have made participation possible at a wide scale beyond previous limitations of influence or social prestige. The stage for public discourse and highly visible expression has grown to a massive scale and everyone, it seems, has been invited.

As illustrated in the previous chapters, our findings have shown exposure to online hate to be a prominent part of the online experience globally, especially among those highly active online. In this chapter we examine the increasingly stratified role of hate in the everyday context in more detail, along with the potential implications that this type of development may have in the future. We also introduce new theoretical tools for examining negative behaviour in the online context, to better explain why hate has become, in many ways, a new norm in online discussions. As noted before, many of the existing theoretical frameworks are based on offline behaviour. It is therefore necessary to strengthen existing approaches by providing new tools to understand negative online behaviour. Here, this is done by updating understandings of the behaviour and risk environment given in past work by including factors central to the unique characteristics of the current online environment.

7.2 Internet and the stratification of hate

Over the past two decades or so, the social sphere of hate has been highly influenced by the Internet. As already noted in previous chapters, hate-motivated groups were among the first to turn to the Internet in their efforts to get their message across. Instead of merely occupying a street corner and handing out flyers to occasional random strangers, the Internet has made it possible to expand the social sphere of any particular cause by connecting with other like-minded people. As a result, the social sphere of hate took its first steps towards greater stratification.

Now, obviously the same transformation applies to a whole host of other ideologies and interests as well and not merely to those motivated by hate. The Internet and social media have created individualised platforms for all kinds of causes, thus in part also explaining why hate has become a somewhat common aspect of the everyday social sphere due to high levels of interaction, visibility and topical overlap. In other words, hate is in many ways just like any other cause or ideology relying on the online social platform, and this in part explains why it often blends into the everyday online narrative of so many.

So what do we mean when we talk about the stratification of hate? Let us focus on this question for a moment. To start with, nature provides a helpful example in conceptualising this development. Just as trees comprise rings that add a new layer of growth every year, building on the foundation of past growth, so too hate has seen a new type of layer emerge every time technology experiences a spike in development. The result is a stratification online hate, as seen in Figure 7.1.

In concrete terms, the central and oldest layer is made up of traditional hate groups that are still active offline and online. These groups continue to maintain websites that inform their audience of their basic ideology, grant access to comment sections on news or related events, and provide information regarding

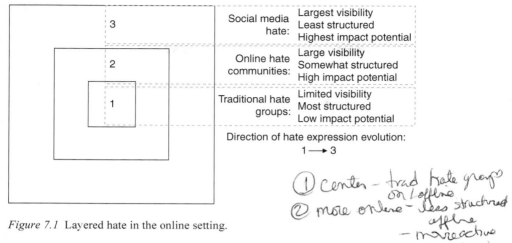

	Social media hate:	Largest visibility Least structured Highest impact potential
	Online hate communities:	Large visibility Somewhat structured High impact potential
	Traditional hate groups:	Limited visibility Most structured Low impact potential

Direction of hate expression evolution:
1 ⟶ 3

Figure 7.1 Layered hate in the online setting.

[handwritten margin notes: ① center – trad hate groups on/offline ② more online – less structured offline – more reactive draw. ③ social media – less managed]

potential social gatherings, protests and so forth. These websites typically have only a handful of visitors and a relatively small following due to the necessity for audiences to search specifically for a particular site. The second layer comprises online hate communities, such as stormfront.org, which tend to be less structured at a strictly physically operational level while also being more active online. They tend to have a much larger following and a much more influential role among like-minded users, being more active in drawing in attracted participants. Finally, in the third and newest layer are social media. Now, this is by far both the most visible sphere for hate and its expression and the least structured, as it is both highly platform-driven and user-driven. Here, a multitude of users are all granted a high level of visibility for expression relatively free from the management or restrictions of an enforcing community as can be the case with the other layers. As the scale of the layer grows, so too does influence, audience size, and the degree to which expression or group identity is unstructured.

What is notable is that each of these stratified layers represents a different layer of the web societies we introduced in the first chapter, thus serving as an illustration of the evolving social spheres of hate. One of the effects brought about by the Internet is that the visibility of hate has increased significantly. This then begs the question: have people become more hateful in general, or is it merely a question of having a wider-reaching public outlet for hate that has always existed? The new channels of communication facilitated by the evolution of the Internet have resulted in a growth in highly polarised environments for general discussion and debate, due to a high level of access to like-minded others and groups accessible for targeting, combined with a visible platform from which expression can be given the desired level of identifiability and visibility.

[handwritten margin note: more hate? or greater comm. outlets for hate]

Often, discussions can result in stronger negative messages than was perhaps originally intended, as the communication environment available today for public expression of opinion can create a spiralling, almost vacuum-like, sphere where rapid escalation is possible. Here, a moment of reactionary expression can grow into something much more damaging. It can start from something as small as a careless tweet, like Justine Sacco's infamous "Going to Africa. Hope I don't get AIDS. Just kidding. I'm white!" This quickly stirred social media into a frenzy. This misstep eventually resulted in her losing her job while drowning in a sea of tens of thousands of hate-filled messages from strangers around the world. Justine Sacco claimed her tweet was intended as an ironic statement of the existing class differences between the Western world and developing nations rather than as a racist remark. Regardless of initial intent, the pace and scale of escalation in this example represent a new phenomenon of relatively small actions taking hold online and creating significant consequences. Context rarely counts for much when things get out of control in social media, whether in a positive or a negative sense. Now, it would be easy to argue that this is simply the fundamental nature of the pace of interaction that exists in social media. However, it is possible that the online setting takes certain behaviours that already exist offline to a higher level by providing a platform, access and even relative safety that may not be available otherwise.

7.3 Evolution of online hate

The wider societal environment is continually influenced by a host of different factors and world events. In particular, major global crises such as the economic crisis of 2008, which was followed by major challenges in the economic market and employment sector throughout the world, or the continuous conflict in the Middle East which has ultimately resulted in mass migration to many parts of Europe, are examples of events that influence the societal dialogue of a very large community. However, there are also more targeted events, such as terrorist attacks, that have a similar impact. A common denominator of many of these events is that they result in increasingly polarised dialogue and communication within social media online.

Events such as the Arab Spring in 2010 have been highly influenced by the tools of the online setting, and even dubbed "the social media revolution" due to the relatively visible role of different social media tools. Here, Twitter was especially active in broadcasting what was happening on the ground. Although the role of social media in actually mobilising the Arab Spring demonstrations has perhaps been overstated, the Internet, and social media specifically, do have a highly influential role in providing a rapid and visible outlet for information, whether from conflict zones, for example during the annexation of Crimea by the Russian Federation in 2014, or in the 2016 presidential election campaign in the US. In addition to simply sharing information, various social media tools have a significant role in shaping attitudes and the expression of different opinions and narratives. Now, the challenge of this combination of high levels of data and visibility is that, in many cases, the audience remains ignorant as to whether the content provided is actually accurate and factual as it is being produced quickly in massive quantities.

One thing that has become increasingly evident is that biases are prominent in the flow of information in terms of determining content, its dissemination rate and level of visibility. Much of the content disseminated on social media that ends up being consumed globally cannot necessarily be separated from the views, background and experiences of the content producer due to the lack of an external filtering process. This freedom to express without external account-ability can result in a cycle that entrenches personal viewpoints without a process of contrast involving perhaps beneficial counterpoints. This helps to explain the polarising communication environment where users insist on strengthening already held views during interaction or content production. Where the chances of encountering other points of view are limited, so too may be the potential for personal growth and development in processing information and other self-motivating content.

7.4 The online user experience and expression of hate

The social environment visible today in the global context in terms of social unrest and aggression tends to be mirrored increasingly in the online world. The online platforms available to all users, from those seeking different sources of entertainment to those motivated to target certain people or groups, are remark-ably diverse. The tools available there can be used to hide one's identity or to make it known to the world. The experience can be tailored by individual prefer-ence in ways that were impossible only a few years ago. Unsurprisingly, this level of flexibility can be used for both harmful and beneficial purposes depend-ing on the user in question. But how did we get here? What are the most relevant components of the online user experience that illustrate the immense shifts in the development of the Internet as a platform for expression?

Figure 7.2 illustrates the steps that the online experience has taken. There have been a series of shifts involving changes in focus but past structures have been maintained. The framework of the Internet builds upon itself, adding fea-tures and interactive possibilities along with the various tools that can be used in new ways. Not long ago, the Internet was primarily a convenient library of information. It was a place to find content from the comfort of one's home. This represented a revolutionary shift in access to content. Yet, looking back, the amount of content available then would be considered minuscule by any standard when compared to what we have today. The early years of Internet use were focused on this content retrieval. Consumption of this content was passive, as one rarely had the possibility of interacting with it or with other users for that matter. Back then, self-expression online was minimal as access to content cre-ation was so limited.

Today, having an online identity is as normal as having a mobile phone. This is especially true of younger generations, born after the late 1980s. Many ques-tions related to individuals' identities were different during the information web stage, with the online world being more clearly separated from the offline self. An online self was an irrelevant concept due to the lack of interactive tools or

The information web	The social web	The integrated web
Low content creation	Moderate content creation	High content creation
Passive consumption	Active consumption	Continual active consumption
Limited self-expression platform	Growing self-expression platform	Global self-expression platform
Slow-paced content feedback loop	Fast-paced content feedback loop	Instant content feedback loop
Lack of online identity	Partially immersed online identity	Fully immersed online identity
Low offline vs online self overlap	Moderate offline vs online self overlap	High offline vs online self overlap

Figure 7.2 The evolution of online user experience.

[handwritten margin notes: Initially kept separate on the web / Selves separate / now integrated]

the possibility of identity creation in the setting. The Internet was a place to visit, explore and learn. It was not a place to connect with others, whether for destructive purposes or otherwise. However, this was about to change and that change brought an incredible array of social tools.

The emergence of the social web was also revolutionary, building on the previous content retrieval functions while boosted by the technical developments of social media platforms. This combination of the possibility of content creation and the ability to create an online persona opened the floodgates to online expression. Here, consumption shifted from passive to active. Users were no longer bound to rigid one-way content interaction, as content could now be modified and created through any number of social platforms. Feedback loops between users and content shifted into a faster gear, as reactions could now be expressed online. From Wikipedia and YouTube to Facebook and online interest-based communities, the social and expressional aspects of the Internet exploded.

Social networking sites allowed users to seamlessly extend their offline relationships and selves online, though still separated by a screen. This shift created a new dynamic, namely an overlapping of the online and offline self. Visibility online can carry significant risks, as one's identifiable characteristics can be targeted by others, whether known or strangers. As covered in previous chapters, the most common targets of online hate have to do with physical appearance, sexual orientation, ethnicity and religious background. If users present themselves with identifying characteristics online, they may potentially experience hate due to the visibility of those online personas in social media, for example. The global nature of the platform combined with heightened ease of access to others has proved damaging to many users cross-nationally. Added to this, the platforms in question here do not require users to prove their identities. As such, the creation of an online self could be an exaggerated version of the self in any number of ways while aggressors are also protected from accountability. Appearance, personal history, expressed interests and personality can now all be modified for the first time in a setting where others cannot be sure of their accuracy in the offline setting. This ability to customise self-presentation and one's interactive network can be used for both positive and destructive goals. Increased access to others, the ability to create an alternate persona through a profile or username and the capacity for seeking out like-minded users from all over the world have created a user-generated content market on a scale never before seen and whose negative effects have been felt globally in terms of targeted hate content.

Gradual shifts in both technology and online platforms available have since begun to take these developments of the social web even further. We have moved towards an integration of online and offline, where connection does not necessarily end but rather is modified into various modes of online self. Here online self and offline self, as identifying terms, become less relevant as the overlap between them grows. Furthermore, content creation is continual to a global audience. Expression can be effectively targeted and visibility can be heightened through numerous global content channels. Making a comfortable living from starting a video blog channel on YouTube would have been a strange concept just ten years ago. The market for content is accelerating towards saturation; the ease of access and the availability of interactive partners giving feedback concerning content have changed the way media are consumed and delivered.

A process began whereby the online experience was tailored to the individual user, instead of the other way around. Google, YouTube and a great host of other service providers work to ensure that advertising, entertainment content and search results match our past browsing and consumption patterns. The online environment has begun adapting itself to the needs, desires and past preferences of users in terms of content offered to meet the individual in the online setting. This is a case of developing bubbles of influence around our preferences in order to provide a more enjoyable experience online. However, with positive cycles comes the possibility of negative cycles as well. Those seeking validation for destructive causes and intentions will find it online, and the online environment can in turn reinforce these consumption patterns to match user preference.

This evolution of the Internet has been one of significant change in terms of expression and scope of influence. We are at the point where personal views can be expressed to a global audience with a minimal filtering process. There are of course amazing benefits to such freedom of expression, but also serious costs. These costs, or risks, of the tools offered by the online setting when combined with users seeking to cause targeted harm, are enabled by the ease of content creation, the convenience of reaching a massive global audience and the potential to limit one's identifiability throughout the process. These three components of methods, scope and control of visibility are central to the creation of a useful model of the online hate dynamics prevalent today.

7.5 New theoretical tools for examining online hate

The online setting and expression within it function on the same principles as have been apparent in the offline setting for decades. The individual does not become someone entirely different when consuming and creating online content, despite significant variations in access to others, customisable self-presentation and high content availability. The Internet is popular in large part for the interaction it makes available, namely access to like-minded others in search of validation and acceptance (Allen, Szwedo & Mikami, 2012; Davidson & Martelozzo, 2013). Furthermore, the Internet as an interactive setting has certain risk factors built into the way interaction takes place. Three primary frameworks were implemented to illustrate the relevant frames of reference in the study of identity, the online setting and risk thus far. These frameworks were Social Identity Theory (SIT) (Tajfel & Turner, 1979), the social identity model of deindividuation effects (SIDE) (Lea & Spears, 1991) derived from that theory, and Lifestyle Exposure Theory (LET) (Hindelang, Gottfredson & Garofalo, 1978) and Routine Activity Theory (RAT) (Cohen & Felson, 1979), involving risk patterns and environmental factors related to them.

As was noted, portions of each framework are highly relevant to the online setting. In the case of social identity theory, group formation through shared identity characteristics and the need for validation are clearly present in the online setting where all manner of social support and shared-interest groups abound. There, group formation becomes easier than ever, as finding a specific shared ideology or interest is conveniently searchable. Furthermore, the identity group prototype, or the generalised and idealised member of a given group, can hold sway online as well as in the setting of a standard of behaviour or attitude while also enhancing the strength of group bonds. Online, users have access to all manner of identity prototypes including details of their lives and ideologies. From sports, film and music stars to war heroes, politicians and founders of hate movements – everyone can find something that they would like to be inspired by, matching their intent with like-minded behaviour personified by prototypical examples.

The phenomenon of depersonalisation is particularly relevant in the online setting in terms of identity theory. Creation of an identity group involves a process of perspective management where thinking moves from the individual self to the group self. In other words, when interacting online, users are more likely to represent a viewpoint or preferred characteristic. Here, individual complexity is abandoned in favour of self-stereotyping to act as a representative of group norms, a process often strengthened by the example of an identity prototype. This framework helps to explain the intense and often aggressive interactions involving race, politics or religion, for example, that take place in the comment sections of cat videos and entertainment news articles. Online, entrenched views seem to clash more aggressively and escalate more quickly than is typical offline. There is an environmental factor built into the online setting that helps to account for this.

These phenomena are active in all group identity formation situations as presented by social identity theory, but the SIDE model takes the discussion further by showing that the online setting provides an additional characteristic that may intensify the effect of depersonalisation. As the online setting involves a lower level of social presence, both identifiability and visibility can be altered. Online, a user can choose how easily he or she can be identified in addition to how visible he or she is physically. This carries significant effects in three primary areas, namely expression, self-presentation and exploration. In terms of expression, lessened social presence can encourage higher levels of disclosure and overall interaction (see, for example, Ferriter, 1993). This phenomenon is heightened online where visibility and identifiability can be controlled. Being physically removed from the interaction encourages users to say and do more in the online setting, opening up fuller communication. This tendency holds even in cases where interacting partners are already known to one another and thus easily identifiable (Joinson, 2001; Keipi & Oksanen, 2014).

In terms of controlling identifiability, the ability to hide oneself online can encourage more openness due to the potential for remaining unknown to the interacting partner. This social invisibility can encourage users to express things they would otherwise be afraid to, as any judgement received will not be traced back to them offline. Online, users can express identity characteristics in ways relatively free from external norms and constraints as group norm enforcement is diminished in certain environments. Here, tough guys can enjoy modes of entertainment that would be mocked if their identity group peers were aware of them; members of political groupings can explore topics and discussions likely to be hindered by offline relationships (Keipi & Oksanen, 2014). This relative freedom from external constraints can of course be highly beneficial to both social development and identity reinforcement. However, the opposite may also be the case. Users harbouring latent racism or xenophobia, for example, may strengthen those views online by seeking out settings in which to produce targeted content without fear of being found out.

A second aspect of exploration is that of customising oneself in order to gain acceptance online. The online setting, combined with some level of lessened social presence, allows users to customise the way they are perceived. Namely, users can create profiles, avatars and usernames that reflect a desired version of the self that is more attractive to a sought-after group. Due to the possibility of customising one's online self, the process of seeking validation from certain identity groups can be accelerated, especially when users are knowledgeable about group norms and identity prototype characteristics. Profiles, interests, attitudes and appearance can all be presented in a way that users feel would be most attractive to a desired identity group, thus assisting in the pursuit of group validation and acceptance (Anderson, Fagan, Woodnutt & Chamorro-Premuzic, 2012; Chew, LaRose, Steinfield & Velasquez, 2011). This customised self-presentation facilitated by lessened social presence online allows for identity exploration that would otherwise be practically impossible. Online, gender roles, identity group affiliations, cultural attitudes, political views and all aspects of personal history and reputation can be manipulated or simply created in whatever way users want. This change of identity is something unique to the online setting where certain versions of the self can be explored through interaction and resulting reactions in order to form a more complete picture of one's identity. Online, playing devil's advocate is convenient and even easy. Exploring what it might be like to be of a different gender, sexual preference or religious tradition can have profound effects on users who are able to experience some small portion of those identities in the online setting while also gaining desired support in the process.

These group identity dynamics and enhancements made possible in the online setting also apply for harmful communities. Hate online can be aggressive and identities tied to its forms can grow and even thrive where validation and group culture are actively maintained. As the Internet has developed into the social and expressional matrix it now is, so too has the creation of hate material and the formation of hate groups. Early on, hate material was indeed available to users in lesser quantities. Information can be dangerous in motivating aggression through, for example, making targets identifiable or providing group validation for destructive action. The scope of both access and content online allows for an interactive stage that can magnify these processes. Not only is that same information available in greater quantities with easier access, social reinforcement of its norms abound, in addition to the availability of active identity prototypes and similar social groups. Message boards, video content, social networking events and all manner of fan pages continually add to the damaging content and identity conceptions adopted by users seeking these characteristics and attitudes. The online environment has thus evolved into a place where risk is prevalent and threat prevention is difficult.

7.6 The interaction between aggressors and targets online

We can find examples of practically every type of person, interest and perception online. Often, those most visible are those most aggressive in giving expression that causes controversy or damage. These high-impact interactions occur continually in many ways online where targets of hate or other discrimination are easily accessible. When we think about a risky situation where an aggressor targets a potential victim, three primary components come into play in terms of how likely victimisation is to occur according to both LET and RAT, with the focus here on the latter. First, how easily can a victim be accessed by the aggressor? If an individual is seeking a certain target for harassment or other abuse, a low cost of entry into that interaction will motivate that negative action. Second, how motivated is the offender? A number of factors play into the decision to cause harm that is easier to do online. Third, how well is the potential victim protected from harm? Good protection is more difficult to bypass and therefore diminishes the likelihood of damaging action.

Past theories have analysed these components in the offline setting in order to assess experiences of victimisation in daily life (Cohen & Felson, 1979; Hindelang et al., 1978; Miethe & Meier, 1990; Reyns, Henson & Fisher, 2011). However, as we have seen, the social setting available online is vastly different from the offline setting in a number of significant ways: ways that can make aggression easier and therefore more likely, for example in terms of cyberbullying, malware attacks, identity theft and other forms of victimisation (e.g. Holt & Bossler, 2009; Holt, Bossler, Malinski & May, 2016; Kigerl, 2011; Leukfeldt & Yar, 2016; Näsi, Oksanen, Keipi & Räsänen, 2015; Pratt, Holtfreter & Reisig, 2010). Figure 7.3 provides a comparison of key areas relating to how this aggressor–victim dynamic has evolved through the tools available online. However, there exists little unifying theory on how the risk environment has changed given the unique characteristics of the online setting and so a great deal of room for interpretation exists.

In the offline setting where most human interaction has taken place historically, reaching a suitable target carries a relatively high cost, which is made up of a number of factors. First, the offender is physically present. Voice and appearance are easily identified by the victim or by other witnesses of the interaction or attack. Therefore offender and victim converge in the same place at the same time. Second, in the offline setting, physical interaction brings the potential for physical protection by witnesses or other environmental factors. The interaction, occurring in a physical space, may be witnessed by unexpected sources of assistance. Furthermore, the likelihood of abuse may be apparent before the incident occurs, judged by situational awareness, physical surroundings and suspicious behaviour. There is the potential for many cues to be leveraged as warning signs by the suspecting victim. The offender makes decisions based on

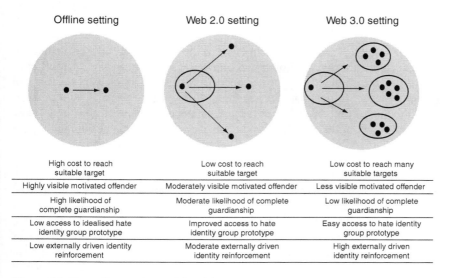

Offline setting	Web 2.0 setting	Web 3.0 setting
High cost to reach suitable target	Low cost to reach suitable target	Low cost to reach many suitable targets
Highly visible motivated offender	Moderately visible motivated offender	Less visible motivated offender
High likelihood of complete guardianship	Moderate likelihood of complete guardianship	Low likelihood of complete guardianship
Low access to idealised hate identity group prototype	Improved access to hate identity group prototype	Easy access to hate identity group prototype
Low externally driven identity reinforcement	Moderate externally driven identity reinforcement	High externally driven identity reinforcement

Figure 7.3 The online routine activity risk spectrum.

the various characteristics of a potential victim and the situation itself, while environmental characteristics also play a role. Is the goal of the targeting valuable? How able is the target to put up an effective defence or to deter harmful action? How accessible is the target to the offender and how easily can they be noticed? Finally, how accessible is an escape route for the offender? These questions are central to the determination of aggressor action.

From the point of view of an aggressor, a lessening of these costs of the desired damaging behaviour makes the negative expression more likely. In the online setting, the physical nature of abuse is lessened due to the lack of physical interaction as a whole. This benefits the online aggressor. However, expression and communication are still very much alive and well online, enhanced to a degree impossible offline, and their damaging effects should not be underestimated. Low cost of entry into abuse can widen the scope of negative action significantly. Online abuse is thus an immense problem whose mechanisms are well known yet lack a complementary theoretical model to explain them. This is the starting point for the potential risks enabled by the online medium of interaction.

Here, the costs of reaching a suitable target are minimal as the entire global web is accessible from one's location. Furthermore, the available tools for self-presentation and identity creation can be used to minimise one's identifiability and visibility. This lessening of accountability can be leveraged to motivate action that might otherwise be avoided due to external pressure or the effect on reputation (Keipi & Oksanen, 2014). If an individual has decided to seek out a target only if identifiability can be prevented, the online setting is ideal as it eliminates both concerns. Online, users can display themselves as they wish in order to interact with any number of known or unknown persons.

When it comes to preventing victimisation, certain precautions can be taken online and offline. Offline, as mentioned, the physical nature of an offence may provide warning as to the likelihood of aggression may be. Online, however, cues are often unavailable due to the nature of interaction there. Furthermore, the nature of content online is different from in the offline world. Users can create all manner of offensive and otherwise damaging material in the form of texts, videos and images that can be posted and shared throughout all avenues of social media. Exposure to this material is difficult to prevent if users spend any significant amount of time browsing online and interacting in spaces considered safe, as was reflected in the findings of previous chapters in terms of the high rate of hate targeting and content exposure. This potential for accidental exposure is a phenomenon that has really taken off in the online setting. In these cases, the original creator of content may or may not have had a specific target in mind. Whatever the original intent, the exposure of the damaging content can expand well beyond the social circles for which it was meant. As such, the level of damage from material may be best measured not by the intensity of the intent behind its creation but by the mechanisms by which it is spread and shared. This raises an interesting aspect of the online environment: namely, the like-minded advocates who are ready and willing to spread damaging targeted material without being asked to do so by the creator. Access to others sharing similar hatreds or negative perceptions online is readily available and so the potential for widespread help in disseminating the sentiment is also there.

Finally, the structural components of the online setting are most effective in modelling behaviour when they are matched to characteristics of interaction that we all share, namely social identity. Validation, acceptance, developing a sense of self and expressing sentiments are significant components of our functioning in a social identity space (Abrams & Hogg, 2004; Jenkins, 2004; Tajfel & Turner, 1979; Thoits, Virshup, Lauren & Ashmore, 1997). All of this is also true of those active in targeted hate. Hate groups, focused communities, previously published material and personally created material are all accommodated by various forms of social media available today. Not only are the aforementioned identity prototypes for various identity groups readily available for study and inspiration, but the environment itself can actively reinforce the damaging perceptions of hate. Both aggressors and victims associate themselves with certain social identities, from certain music styles to political affiliations and religious practices. This is all done through individual motivation. But with development comes change, often through contrasting views and perspectives. However, this change may be prevented and damaging perspectives reinforced if the social setting is tailored to cater to individuals' current interests and past preferences. Here, individuals and groups they associate with can become immersed in self-reinforcing cycles online.

Notably, as has been stressed throughout, the online social setting is global and as such many characteristics and dynamics of interaction are shared. However, the application and outcome of theory and modelling of these issues will naturally have different implications in different countries and cultural contexts. Here, we focus on what we consider universal characteristics whose more specific dynamics may differ depending on the individuals in question. As such, the frameworks of social identity online including implications of validation, depersonalisation, self-presentation, visibility and identifiability, in addition to risk factors of accessibility to others, potential for minimising accountability and capacity for defence against offenders are considered broadly applicable. Indeed, how and to what extent these components play out in the online context can vary a great deal.

7.7 Identity Bubble Reinforcement model (IBR model)

As we have noted above, we can use some of the existing theoretical frameworks applied generally in the offline context to try to understand hate in the online context as well. However, it is also evident due to recent developments in the online setting that a deeper understanding of the Internet and the interactions it facilitates would benefit from a lens calibrated for these new phenomena. One such lens that focuses on how the online environment can affect the individual user is what call as the Identity Bubble Reinforcement model (IBR model).

At the core of this new IBR model are mechanisms of exposure to online content and identity dynamics. In order to understand better what we mean by

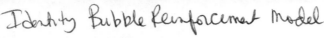

this we need to return to the beginning of this book. In the first chapter, we provided an overview of how the modern-day online information, or network, society, came to be. New markets have emerged, resulting in massive leveraging of information. The key revenue model of online giants such as Google and Facebook allows them to provide targeted ads based on users' online behaviour. This type of business logic is based on the fact that companies such as Google and Facebook actively collect data on each Internet user's online behaviour, including their particular interests, purchasing habits, specific content search patterns, news provider preferences, categories of information interests, interacting partners, timeframes of high interaction, and so forth. What these companies are essentially doing is creating a consumption-based profile of each individual using their services. Based on this profile, users can be targeted with content that they may be interested in. From a sociological and social psychological perspective, a customised environment of this sort carries interesting implications in terms of how individuals develop socially.

There are a number of different factors that contribute to the popularity of various social media platforms. On the one hand there is the chance to communicate and share important aspects of one's life with others, while on the other hand social media provide useful tools for both social identity reflection and construction. From a theoretical perspective, our interest is focused on these social identity dynamics. By liking certain content or posting certain pictures, users promote a certain version of the self that is in the process of being developed or is already complete and ready to be presented to the online world as they see fit. Now, this social identity construction is a two-way street. Users are commonly influenced by the different content that they come across online, which in part also influences their own social identity formation. Therefore, the social identity displayed by users online can be customised to a high degree depending on user motivations. The Internet is thus a highly controlled environment in terms of how one wishes to be perceived, enabling a much more constructed self-projection than is possible in offline situations.

A carefully constructed picture of your Sunday morning breakfast, including a bowl filled with fresh berries, a power smoothie made from kale, kiwis and bananas, and a freshly brewed cup of coffee, portrays an image of healthy living. Posting a picture on one's Instagram account displaying views from a Sunday afternoon run carries a similar message. Sharing a picture on a night out with friends projects a message of social connections and of living an exciting and fun life. From projecting health, popularity, success or any number of other desired characteristics, social media can be used to advertise aspects of the self in new ways. These are just a few examples of how easy it has become to manage our self-image through convenient control of how users are experienced by a social network. When users interact, post pictures or thoughts, add links and share interests, a process of creating a version of themselves online takes shape perhaps in the hope of validation and socially desirability. In many ways, social media provide tools for cataloguing ourselves, often with the purpose of expressing who we are and to ensure that others know the things about us that we have chosen that they should know. This is an interesting dynamic, as it involves a high level of control over the perceptions of others and can be a powerful tool indeed, both for meeting personal needs and for enjoying the company of others with similar interests.

We tend to like those who like us and who also like the same things as we do; no surprise there. But what about cases where growth and personal development are dependent on contrast and even conflict between viewpoints that do not agree? Do we, as individuals, always know what is best for us in terms of what we choose to connect with others over? This high level of managing one's own networks is of course a great and healthy resource if we are making healthy decisions in terms of how we connect and what interests we invest in.

Many aspects of ourselves, or our social identities, are harmless or carry a positive effect in terms of our wellbeing. We enjoy interacting and sharing things that are important to us, from hobbies to relationships and professions to habits. But what happens in instances where an individual is driven to aggressively target certain people, groups or individuals? How we present ourselves online affects who is attracted to our persona there. Communities form around a shared vision, and if that vision is one of causing harm, a great deal of risk to others can result. Tendencies to racist views, for example, can grow from occasional thoughts to damaging action when destructive identities are reinforced through accepted norms and prototypical examples among respected group members. Specific targeting of certain groups was also prominent in our data, as characteristics of ethnic background, religious belief and physical appearance were all leading points of contact at which hate was targeted by users of opposing identity groups.

Furthermore, it should be noted that less socially acceptable attitudes and perceptions tend to be difficult to develop offline where such communities tend not to advertise. However, those seeking to connect over racism or other hate-based attitudes online are provided with any number of ways to validate beliefs, interact over experiences or connect through specific types of communication that would otherwise be problematic. In addition, in this setting one need not hide behind a majority to motivate hateful content against a weaker minority, as safety can be created by limiting visibility or identifiability and achieving similar results. Online, the broader social context does not filter content or regulate behaviour to the same extent as offline. Rather, identity groups online can regulate themselves, with shared norms and attitudes on which those norms are based. Thus, online, the user can filter out everything but the specifically motivated target towards which he or she wishes to move. The way the Internet is structured in terms of social possibilities allows for a huge variety of unique and even unusual groups and affiliations to form. In a sense, it can cater to everyone in the way they wish to be catered to while also allowing users to be as regulated by group norms as they wish, resulting in complex identity affiliations and memberships. Notably, as a social landscape, the Internet may even be more diverse than what is available offline due to the acceptance of like-minded users into communities that might not dare meet in a setting where they might be identified.

model explained (handwritten margin)

All of these components of the mechanisms of the online environment, individual expression, identity exploration and seeking social validation, come together in the IBR model, illustrated in Figure 7.4.

Here, the external frames represent the scope of the online environment within which the user can seek out, create and consume content. This model is concerned with the consumption patterns and resulting development of the user specifically, though this does link to content creation itself as well. Here, the various shapes represent interests that resonate with the identity landscape of the user. The bubble within the frame is the individual, with the thickness of the bubble representing the strength of a social identity. In the left-hand frame, the individual user holds already prevalent identity characteristics and is thus motivated to seek out similar sources of reinforcing content or interactions online. Notably, a mix of identity characteristics is already present within the individual. As such, no user is completely defined as having one lone identity. Even the most intense members of certain groups can be sons, fathers, mothers, sports fans or musicians, holding any number of other identity group affiliations.

As user-driven identity reinforcement or exploration takes place, the user represents a version of the self at the point of departure into this new interactive framework. Some may be more certain than others of who he or she is as a person. Some go out determined to strengthen who they already feel they are while others may be driven by the desire to find out what is out there to be explored. The validation component of social identity processes is central here, as expression in the online setting tends to heighten identity group characteristics as described by the SIDE model (Lea & Spears, 1995). Here, self-stereotyping

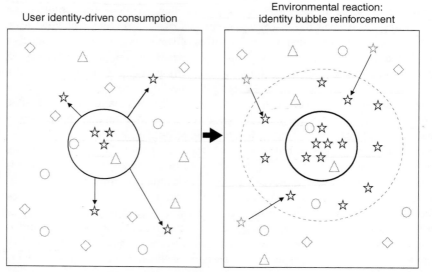

User identity-driven consumption

Environmental reaction:
identity bubble reinforcement

Figure 7.4 The Identity Bubble Reinforcement (IBR) model.

from the aforementioned depersonalisation can motivate an intensified process of classifying oneself according to the contrasting material and interactions one faces. Furthermore, exploring online in order to connect on a certain identity may strengthen that identity through access to various identity prototypes on whom behaviour can be modelled.

All of this has to do with patterns of online consumption driven by the reinforcing desires of the users themselves, each with unique motivations and needs. However, as mentioned earlier, the Internet today is more active than before. In the right-hand frame of the model the environment itself responds to the consumption patterns registered by users. This adaptation in how the Internet functions has significant implications in terms of how identity is reinforced. If the environment responds to the behaviours linked to who we were while seeking certain things in the past by providing more of the same, how is development affected? The fainter bubble in the right-hand frame represents how access to online content is adjusted. It is not that other content is impossible to reach, but rather that the various mechanisms inherent in popular online platforms begin to filter content according to what the user is likely to prefer based on past behaviour. This creates an interesting identity development environment where the users' original intentions are, perhaps unknowingly, reinforced externally accentuate the identified affiliation. This strengthening is represented in the model with the thickening of the bubble as consumption patterns continue to be reinforced by both the individual and the environment itself.

This inherently structured mechanism of reinforcing past behaviours online limits access to contrasting and other points of view that might contradict consumption patterns of the past, often without the knowledge of the users themselves. This can be particularly convenient in terms of matching advertising and search results to things one enjoys. A tailored profile on which the online environment reacts to projected needs may be a good thing. However, socially damaging identity group affiliations and resulting behaviours are a different matter. Here, both the individual and the environment work together to reinforce negative conceptions. Reinforcement of online hate is particularly concerning due to the heightened potential for the effective dissemination of those sentiments.

Furthermore, the issue of cognitive bias (Tversky & Kahneman, 1974) comes into play in an environment that tailors itself to the user in question. Here, cognitive bias refers to reinforcing patterns of norms or decision-making that move one away from a previous reasonable standard. As the online environment adjusts to the user, cognitive bias, or the subjective social reality of the user, can be enhanced further than might otherwise be possible. As input is fed to the user according to his or her points of view, the benefits of objective contrast become less likely. This can take various forms, from an ambiguity effect where certain possibilities are avoided due to lack of information through environmental filtering (Frisch & Baron, 1988), to excessive anchoring or relying too strongly on a limited set of information in decision-making (Kahneman & Tversky, 1996). Furthermore, in the identity group setting, an availability cascade can occur, where shared attitudes or beliefs come to seem increasingly reasonable through shared repetition of norms, for example (Hasher, Goldstein & Toppino, 1977). This strengthening of biases by an environment can lead to both relational and individual damage as perception and decision-making move from being rational and balanced to being subjective and self-reinforcing in any number of ways. Online, active users are more likely to navigate within already established environmentally designated profiles based on past habits, representing a new frontier of bias creation and reinforcement. Although the environmental adjustment to user preference does not cause behaviour, it can certainly affect cycles of consumption and the motivations behind them.

Those seeking community, expression or simply information may be in a vulnerable state where content and interaction have a significant motivating effect whether in positive or negative terms. As users navigate the online setting, some are already motivated to target certain people or groups while others are more interested in seeking validation or identity development of some sort. However, in an environment that reinforces early inputs made by users there exists a unique risk. Namely, there exists the risk of reinforcing an identity bubble that is motivated by some level of user ignorance. Such a bubble can help to pave the way towards further negative behaviour that would have been less likely had the user continued to navigate without an environmental reaction to early patterns. For example, in the case of pro-anorexia content, a user seeking validation for negative processes has convenient access to like-minded others online. Groups encouraging unhealthy decisions reinforce patterns in the user that may have just begun to take root. As patterns of online input are repeated, the users' online behavioural profile takes shape to accommodate those preferences. Here, pro-anorexia communities become even more easily accessible online, with positive feedback affecting the continuation of a negative cycle in the user (Oksanen et al., 2015).

So how do all of these components, from online interactive tools to environmental reactions to those interactions, in addition to social identity theory combined with lifestyle and routine activity risks, fit together with the central theme of online hate? All of these components come together in the individual. The need for validation and development of a stronger self-concept for identity formation drives users to seek out meaning and fulfilment in many ways, especially in the online setting. Many espouse hateful attitudes and perspectives, and therefore seek like-minded groups and content creators with whom to bond or find inspiration. Prototypical idols of various movements are easily accessible, in addition to the countless harmful actions taken by others with whom users may feel bonded. The social tools of customised self-presentation by way of tailored visibility or identifiability can also be leveraged to gain a higher level of acceptance than might otherwise be possible. Here, social needs and an enabling of self-fulfilment overlap with hate networks, leading to an enhancement of tools for identity development in terms of hate. Furthermore, ease of access to expressional platforms combined with a global audience can motivate further activity.

In targeting others with hate content, the cost/benefit calculation in the online setting is different from the offline one. Online, the value of action taken can be maximised due to the ease of access to many potential suitable targets, the ability to control visibility and identifiability, and the high level of produced content exposure combined with a minimal capacity for prevention or defence by victims, and finally the possibility to quickly escape accountability for one's targeting activity. As such, the setting online is well suited to the effective production and dissemination of hate content, while also lacking mechanisms to filter out damaging material whose exposure negatively affects the wellbeing of a global audience.

All of these dynamics are real factors for content producers and their victims in an environment whose immensely valuable tools for communication, expression and connectedness can be used for harmful purposes. But, as discussed, the environment itself also reacts to actions taken by its users. Thus, reinforcement of user preferences is accentuated not only by sophisticated technological tools but also by the behavioural trends interpreted by the environment itself. In terms of hate, this two-pronged reinforcement can operate by both enabling action and limiting exposure to contrasting views, potentially increasingly damaging behavioural cycles.

References

Abrams, D., & Hogg, M. (2004). Metatheory: Lessons from social identity research. *Personality and Social Psychology Review, 8*(2), 98–106. DOI: 10.1207/s15327957pspr0802_2.

Allen, J., Szwedo, D., & Mikami, A. (2012). Social networking site use predicts changes in young adults' psychological adjustment. *Journal of Research on Adolescence, 22*, 453–466. DOI: 10.1111/1532-7795.2012.00788.

Anderson, B., Fagan, P., Woodnutt, T., & Chamorro-Premuzic, T. (2012). Facebook psychology: Popular questions answered by research. *Psychology of Popular Media Culture, 1*, 23–37. DOI: 10.1037/a0026452.

Chew, H., LaRose, R., Steinfield, C., & Velasquez, A. (2011). The use of online social networking by rural youth and its effects on community attachment. *Information, Communication & Society 14*, 726–747. DOI: 10.1080/1369118X.2010.539243.

Cohen, L. E., & Felson, M. (1979). Social change and crime rate trends: A routine activity approach. *American Sociological Review, 44*, 588–608. DOI: 10.2307/2094589.

Davidson, J., & Martelozzo, E. (2013). Exploring young people's use of social networking sites and digital media in the Internet safety context. *Information, Communication & Society, 16*, 1456–1476. DOI: 10.1080/1369118X.2012.701655.

Ferriter M. (1993). Computer aided interviewing and the psychiatric social history. *Social Work and Social Sciences Review 4*, 255–263. DOI: 0.1300/J407v09n01_09.

Frisch, D., & Baron, J. (1988). Ambiguity and rationality. *Journal of Behavioral Decision Making, 1*(3), 149–157.DOI: 10.1002/bdm.3960010303.

Hasher, L., Goldstein, D., & Toppino, T. (1977). Frequency and the conference of referential validity. *Journal of Verbal Learning and Verbal Behavior, 16*(1), 107–112. DOI: 10.1016/S0022-5371(77)80012-1.

Hindelang, M. J., Gottfredson, M. R., & Garofalo, J. (1978). *Victims of Personal Crime: An Empirical Foundation for a Theory of Personal Victimization.* Cambridge, MA: Ballinger. http://dx.doi.org/10.1016/S0022-5371(77)80012-1.

Holt, T. J., & Bossler, A. M. (2008). Examining the applicability of lifestyle-routine activities theory for cybercrime victimisation. *Deviant Behavior, 30*(1), 1–25. DOI: 10.1080/01639620701876577.

Holt, T. J., Bossler, A. M., Malinski, R., & May, D. C. (2016). Identifying predictors of unwanted online sexual conversations among youth using a low self-control and routine activity framework. *Journal of Contemporary Criminal Justice, 32*(2), 108–128. DOI: 10.1177/1043986215621376.

Jenkins, R. (2004). *Social Identity*. London: Routledge.

Joinson, A. (2001). Self-disclosure in computer-mediated communication: The role of self-awareness and visual anonymity. *European Journal of Social Psychology, 31*, 177–192. DOI: 10.1002/ejsp. 36.

Kahneman, D., & Tversky, A. (1996). On the reality of cognitive illusions. *Psychological Review, 103* (3), 582–591. DOI: 10.1037/0033-295X.103.3.582.

Keipi, T., & Oksanen, A. (2014). Self-exploration, anonymity and risks in the online setting: Analysis of narratives by 14–18-year-olds. *Journal of Youth Studies, 17*, 1097–1113. DOI: 10.1080/13676261.2014.881988.

Kigerl, A. (2011). Routine activity theory and the determinants of high cybercrime countries. *Social Science Computer Review*, 0894439311422689. DOI: 10.1177/089443 9311422689.

Lea, M., & Spears, R. (1991). Computer-mediated communication, de-individuation and group decision-making. *International Journal of Man-Machine Studies, 34*(2), 283–301. DOI: 10.1016/0020-7373(91)90045-9.

Lea, M., & Spears, R. (1995). Love at first byte? Building personal relationships over computer networks. In J. Wood & S. Duck (Eds.), *Understudied Relationships: Off the Beaten Track*. Thousand Oaks, CA: Sage.

Leukfeldt, E. R., & Yar, M. (2016). Applying routine activity theory to cybercrime: A theoretical and empirical analysis. *Deviant Behavior*, 1–18. DOI: 10.1080/01639625. 2015.1012409.

Miethe, T. D., & Meier, R. F. (1990). Opportunity, choice, and criminal victimisation: A test of a theoretical model. *Journal of Research in Crime and Delinquency, 27*(3), 243–266. DOI: 10.1177/0022427890027003003.

Näsi, M., Oksanen, A., Keipi, T., & Räsänen, P. (2015). Cybercrime victimization among young people: A multi-nation study. *Journal of Scandinavian Studies in Criminology and Crime Prevention, 16*(2), 203–210. DOI: 10.1080/14043858.2015.1046640.

Oksanen, A., Garcia, D., Sirola, A., Näsi, M., Kaakinen, M., Keipi, T., et al. (2015). Pro-anorexia and anti-pro-anorexia videos on YouTube: Sentiment analysis of user responses. *Journal of Medical Internet Research, 17*. DOI: 10.2196/jmir.5007.

Pratt, T. C., Holtfreter, K., & Reisig, M. D. (2010). Routine online activity and Internet fraud targeting: Extending the generality of routine activity theory. *Journal of Research in Crime and Delinquency, 47*(3), 267–296. DOI: 10.1177/0022427810365903.

Reyns, B. W., Henson, B., & Fisher, B. S. (2011). Being pursued online applying cyber-lifestyle–routine activities theory to cyberstalking victimisation. *Criminal Justice and Behaviour, 38*(11), 1149–1169. DOI: 10.1177/0093854811421448.

Tajfel, H., & Turner, J. C. (1979). An integrative theory of intergroup conflict. *The Social Psychology of Intergroup Relations, 33*(47), 74.

Thoits, P. A., Virshup, L. K., Lauren, K., & Ashmore, R. (1997). Me's and we's: Forms and functions of social identities. In J. Lee (Ed.), *Self and Identity: Fundamental Issues* (pp. 106–133). New York: Oxford University Press.

Tversky, A., & Kahneman, D. (1974). Judgement under uncertainty: Heuristics and biases. *Science 185*, 1124–1131. DOI: 10.1126/science.185.4157.1124.

8 Transformation of social networks and interactions

8.1 Information, anonymity and social networks

Four primary elements make up the core of online societies, namely information, anonymity, social networks and entertainment. For the purpose of this book, entertainment is perhaps slightly less relevant and so it is not included here. On the other hand, we argue that information, anonymity and social networks provide a valuable basis for understanding why hate has become such an influential and visible element in modern-day society.

The original premise of the Internet and its predecessors, such as the Advanced Research Projects Agency Network (ARPANET), was to provide a means and platform for faster and more convenient information exchange. The emphasis here was mainly on scientific or military purposes. Thinking back to this early phase of the Internet, it is difficult to imagine a computer scientist then having the faintest idea of the immense evolution that technologies would enable in the decades to come. The notion of freely shared information on the Internet is really a reflection of the core premise of the sciences in general. Sharing of information is important not only for its potential societal impact; it is also an important part of the validation process for testing any potential findings. Therefore the creation of a network, such as the early Internet, was done largely for the purposes of making this type of interaction more efficient.

However, the notion of free sharing and exchange of information has not been limited to the earlier versions of the Internet; rather it has become the core principle of what the Internet, even after its commercialisation, stands for. Sir Tim Berners-Lee, generally considered the father of the modern Internet, has often noted that the free exchange of information is the core value of the Internet, and that this core value should not be compromised (e.g. Mullin, 2012). However, while this is in many respects a desirable ideology, as the commercialisation of the Internet has continued to progress and billions of people have been introduced as users, it is not particularly surprising that significant challenges have also emerged. From the perspective of information, the printed media have faced major problems due to declining readership since the turn of the millennium. New technology tends to displace previous avenues for products and services. The information available online is in many respects free of charge, directly competing with physical media that require a fee from consumers. This new marketplace for information and interaction online has created an immense number of platforms from which to choose, within which both the benefits and costs of the online setting play out daily.

Besides online content and access being free or significantly less expensive than offline alternatives, the Internet has long been synonymous with anonymity in various forms. Usernames, fake profiles and pseudonyms are all notable parts of online interaction with varying degrees of visibility or identifiability. The purpose of these veiled identities, sometimes varying a great deal from one's more publicly known persona, can be to provide a type of self whose public perception is more manageable. Online anonymity has affected social dynamics by allowing relative freedom from accountability while also encouraging high levels of disclosure and expression without social pressures that might otherwise be present. Some norms are thus less prominent online, where damaging or reactionary behaviours are less subject to control. This new social sphere where rules can be bent through lessened control has also resulted in a mentality that treats online victimisation or targeted hate as less concrete or physical and therefore less significant than offline parallels.

The boundaries between what is considered online and offline have become increasingly transparent with the advent of wide-scale social media and their continuous consumption. Yet, despite this increasing overlap and combining of the online with the offline, it often seems that the old perception of separation remains, as online abuse tends to be considered less serious an issue than offline abuse. One of the reasons for this may be the fact that social control is to an extent less feasible and therefore less evident in the online context. Research has also found, for instance, that lack of eye contact was related to uninhibited and negative behaviour in the online context (Lapidot-Lefler & Barak, 2012). This means that physical presence and identifiability are influential as enforcers of both social interaction and norm control. Indeed, what has come as a bit of a surprise is the fact that even though most social media users interact through their personal profiles, the expected moderating effect of using one's real name and identifiable profile has not been observed. Countless users continue to harass, insult and target others even while online using identities tied to their real names. Thus, even in the absence of anonymity lessened visibility in terms of live physical presence seems to be linked to more extreme levels of expression and disclosure. As such, disguise through anonymity is not a prerequisite to motivating polarising behaviours, although anonymity does seem to make it easier to be harsh and even offensive when those at the receiving end of the message are not actually physically present.

The modern Internet serves as a platform for a countless number of different social networks. Much as in one's "real life", there are different layers to online social networks, some more closely knit than others. Social media have been particularly helpful in making these networks relatively concrete and visible through various linked profiles, with the possibility to socially compare and categorise Facebook friends or Twitter followers, for example. Relational intimacy can be managed with an effectiveness not possible before as social interaction and relationships can be categorised online, and what content, interactions and aspects of the self are visible to different groups can be controlled. In the case of Facebook, for instance, public interactions can be visible to all friends, while capabilities are also available that allow more private connections to take place among a far more limited audience or one on one. As such, one's social life can be visualised and continually updated through the tools provided by social media.

There are also networks that are less concrete and only intersect occasionally. These include interactions stemming from commenting on a particular online news article, media post or video on platforms such as YouTube. Interacting users may not have had any previous connections outside this instance, but they are still linked together through their online actions. Often, these short-term interactions evoke the most extreme behaviour, as can be attested by reading any number of comment sections under otherwise reasonable news stories, personal content posts or videos. Furthermore, although most personal social networks tend traditionally to be based first and foremost on offline connections, the Internet has substantially broadened the scale of social interactions. In the offline context, interaction among the different social networks generally means at least some level of active participation.

However, it is possible to follow a number of different networks from a relatively passive perspective within the online context. That is, one does not necessarily need to engage in actual discussion in order to follow them. Here, we can be connected without being social, lurking and keeping track of who is doing what, whether close friends or merely acquaintances. All the while, users can maintain a high degree of control over how they are perceived through managing online profiles according to personal preferences. As a whole, social media provide an avenue for reinforcing strong relationships already existing offline, creating new ones online or exploring social opportunities through common interests that may not result in any meaningful relationship. This efficiency in interaction and effectiveness in managing and discovering networks offer a new level of both social and identity group development, validation seeking and desired interaction.

8.2 Bubbles and interaction challenges

One of the concepts that stems from research regarding these evolving social networks in the online context is that of bubbles. We briefly discussed some of the basic notions of bubbles in the first chapter of this book, before introducing the Identity Bubble Reinforcement (IBR) model in Chapter 7 in a discussion of social identity development online. In a broader sense, the notion of different online bubbles can be used to illustrate the nature of social interaction in general. Robert Putnam, in his well-known work *Bowling alone: America's declining social capital* (1995), discusses a similar major social shift in the context of bowling. The premise of Putnam's argument is that people have gradually become less engaged in wider social and societal interaction and have instead delved deeper into individualised social space, resulting in a decline in traditional social networks.

The online era has subsequently further extended the process of changing social interactions. While Putnam studied diminishing social connections and societal activity in the light of social evolution, it is evident that social media and their developmental consequences in terms of social networks have had the opposite effect, as they facilitate social connectivity at a potential scale impossible offline. This partial transition from offline to online social interaction is at the core of the current changing social landscape. Non-core social connections, such as those beyond family and close friends, are now occurring more in the online space, rather than through offline avenues. By following one's Facebook newsfeed, all manner of detail is immediately available concerning the lives of the social network, each relationship consisting of varying degrees of closeness yet with similar levels of disclosure and exposure to daily occurrences. Whether old school friends, distant relatives or former colleagues, even distant acquaintances are within reach and potentially part of one's daily online life despite not having a prioritised role in the life of the social media user in question. On the other hand, new social connections constantly emerge as a result of one's online activity. This has also meant that social connections have become more tailormade. For many, less socially present methods of interaction may be preferred, in part because they tend to involve less social pressure and are based on individuals' preferences and schedules. This type of social connection and interaction has become highly manageable online, depending on the disposition and desires of the interacting partners. This development of access and exposure to others has also changed many new social connections from being determined by physical proximity to being based on shared interests.

Online bubbles function to reinforce one's identity by positively affecting preferences and motivations that users display and express. It is important to note that this process is not necessarily a bad thing. Clearly, personalised content and connections as such do not automatically result in negative behaviour. Rather, in many cases the opposite is true. However, problems tend to lie in topics that are more emotionally charged in the general societal context, as they have a tendency to result in polarising behaviour in the online setting. This, in part, has resulted in a present-day social landscape where many traditional social cues have been replaced by aggravated interactions between both individuals and larger social collectives through various facets of social media.

Problems associated with aggravated and even hateful social interactions in the online context have been foregrounded as a notable social issue. What used to be considered a minor negative side-effect of online navigation has now been identified as an illness of its own due to its widespread nature. For instance, the European Commission has recently taken a strong stance against online hate speech and content (European Commission, 2016). The Commission's intention is to make social media companies, such as Facebook, Twitter, Microsoft and YouTube, process complaints regarding hateful content within twenty-four hours. These companies are not only required to act according to their internal policies regarding hate content, but they must also take into consideration national-level legal frameworks. Furthermore, companies are also required to train their staff to counter hate speech and hate content (European Commission, 2016). Indeed, it seems that anti-social behaviour is becoming increasingly regulated in certain markets online.

Given the scope of online content, expression and flexibility, trying to control any of these presents a variety of challenges. To begin with, the core premise of the Internet is strongly resistant to excessive external control that might act to limit expression. Furthermore, in terms of responsibility, there are challenges in motivating companies to invest significant resources in controlling their users, who may in fact leave the service if new, tighter measures of control are implemented. Thus, liability is balanced against profit margins. The case of Edward Snowden revealed wide-scale disapproval of efforts to track online behaviour in the interests of security. The balance of control will be a further challenge in addition to the definition of boundaries. Who will dictate what content is inappropriate and what is not? Who has the final say? Will there be a new punishment system for online violations? These are all questions that need to be addressed when control intensifies.

[handwritten margin note: Controlling users vs profit margins]

8.3 Bringing it all together

In the earlier parts of this book we introduced the notion of cumulating online content. One of our premises was that content, or information, of any type produced or added into the online context tends to cumulate rather than disappear. With billions of worldwide users, this content adds up quickly. One could argue that, in the name of transparency, this is clearly a good thing that keeps everything "out in the open". After all, as mentioned, the central premise of the Internet, the free sharing of information, is based on the notion of transparency. However, there are downsides to storing user content indefinitely. A college student posting drunken content from a house party, a young couple sharing borderline inappropriate and racy pictures from their summer holiday, or an employee abusing his or her boss and the company they work for, all constitute thoughtless actions taken in an instant that result in long-term consequences. In the past, such things may have been remembered for a time, fading away as the content itself was no longer available. Some might carry consequences while others could be hidden or forgotten quickly.

[handwritten margin note: all permanent ↓ good for transparency ↓ bad for long term consequences]

However, what if this content remains accessible, even publicly? What effects would such a possibility carry if, for example, a potential employer in the distant future has access to all of this information? Yes, users can always delete social media posts, or even request that Google delete previous online history if they live in the EU. However, the problem is that these actions alone do not necessarily make all unwanted past content disappear. When the damage is done, and when it is deemed significant enough, the Internet often makes forgetting a difficult and complicated ordeal.

[handwritten note: "... The Internet makes forgetting a difficult + complicated ordeal"]

The core ideology behind the early Internet was the free exchange of information in order to maximise benefits to as large a user base as possible. However, behind the novel core ideology was the presumption that this information would actually be factual and somewhat constructively presented. Thus the resulting interaction would be a reflection of these principles. The cumulating nature of the Internet combined with the massive influx of user-generated data has created a body of content made up of, in large part, personal perceptions, opinions and views, often lacking in facts and structure. Thus, much factual information or discussion can disappear somewhere in the sea of less constructive content. A significant portion of the Internet has become a space fostering misinformation rather than reputable sources. At the heart of the leveraging of misinformation are often those users already entrenched in opposing social identities. This has created a sort of melting pot of different opinions among very different types of people. Continually adding to the undignified nature of much of Internet debate, often not unlike the unfiltered nature of intoxicated interaction, can create a challenging social environment in which navigating between reasonable and highly biased becomes a struggle. Where social norms, physical cues, feedback detection and self-censorship are minimised, so too can be civility and responsible discourse. Here we get to the heart of the problem. In the sea of an endless number of Internet users, in order to be heard, one often has to speak the loudest. In the online context, this tends to mean that those presenting exaggerated content grab attention more effectively than those users who choose to take more constructive or reasonable approaches. The result of all this can be a bias towards polarised views whose proponents are self-selected through the volume they project on the online space.

As stated in Chapter 2 above and our discussion of Social Identity Theory (e.g. Tajfel & Turner, 1979), individuals tend to seek positive self-image through their group memberships. As a result, however, they also tend to view their own group as superior to other groups. This becomes more of an issue in the context of emotionally charged topics as the role of these groups becomes more intensified. Sunstein and Hastie (2015), for instance, have noted that the combination of group membership and an emotionally charged topic has polarised even those with moderate views on the issues in question. Online, where group identities are particularly prominent as a basis for interaction due to depersonalisation (Lea, Spears & de Groot, 2001), there is a great deal of potential for damaging polarisation as norms of civility or mutual respect are disregarded. These social networks act as places of opportunity: opportunity for finding validation, acceptance, new points of view or strengthening self-concept. As these aspects of the self evolve online, affected by both individual needs and environmental reaction to those needs, the global nature of the online space makes conflict and victimisation all the more likely. From the perspective of everyday hate, social networks play a central role. Namely, they can provide users with connections that can in turn be used to help create an illusion of a justified cause, even when based on hate and intolerance. Thus, online tools can act as reinforcing mechanisms that may, in the often polarising environment, result in rapid escalation in negative sentiment or behaviour.

One of the core necessities of a healthy and functioning society is a proper waste management system. Now if we consider waste management not from the perspective of city infrastructure but from the perspective of the Internet, hate-related content could be categorised as the worst kind of waste, namely toxic waste, due to its harmful nature. As most of us know, the problem with toxic waste is that not only is it extremely hazardous to public health, it is also very difficult and costly to dispose of. Therefore, much like nuclear waste, hate and hate content have the potential to remain toxic for years to come due to the difficulty of completely removing past online content.

Looking back to our main findings in Chapters 4, 5 and 6, the effects of this toxicity can be far-reaching, with significant consequences affecting users. Online hate content can have second- and third-degree effects, causing harm to users far beyond the intended scope of the offender. Throughout our findings, those exposed to hate content, whether accidentally or by specific targeting said that the effect on their perceived wellbeing had been clearly negative. Our data naturally show differences between young people in the four countries surveyed, but shared features of the findings are likely the most relevant when thinking of effects on the global scale. Here, hate content does not carry diminishing returns in terms of harm, as the initial negative experience does not lessen the negative experience of others exposed later to the same targeted content.

Thus, if the quantity of online hate content continues to grow, so too will the amount of toxic content that has the potential to further fuel negative interactions and content production. History shows that once highly polarised opinions become the new norm, particularly through the main channels of popular interaction, whether a Speakers' Corner, a political rally or social media, the results are rarely constructive. This is not to say that polarisation automatically results in extreme behaviour, but rather that context and compromise do matter in social discourse and identity development. We are no strangers to polarised views and expressions of hate, having witnessed several massive demonstrations in response to the wave of refugees and mass immigration in Europe, hate-filled dialogue attacking the Muslim community in the current round of the US presidential election, or any number of debates about global warming, feminism, nutrition, vaccinations, and the list goes on. All of these issues which arouse entrenched views are saturating the online setting.

Both hate and toxicity have therefore gained what could be called an everyday presence. What we mean by this is that the expression of hate, targeted disapproval and anti-social behaviour have become so common that they are constantly present in our online landscape. The combination of increasing online interaction and a perceived level of anonymity has led to more extreme and more polarised social debate that is as visible as it is toxic. Our findings show that exposure to hate content has become common, yet only a relatively small number of users admit to having produced such material. What may explain this is that very few users actually perceive themselves as having produced hate content, and simultaneously consider abrasive interaction a normal part of online culture. Nonetheless, even if only a small number individuals are active producers of hate content, the Internet provides them with a potentially global audience and far-reaching negative influence.

8.4 Final reflections

What makes the increased presence of hate in the online landscape perplexing is that hate as such is damaging to both victims and offenders. Research shows that feelings of anger and hate have various negative consequences, ranging from personal and interpersonal problems to stress and physical health problems (Johnson, 1990; Martin, Coyier, VanSistine & Schroeder, 2013; Suls & Bunde, 2005). Therefore, any effort to tackle the presence of hateful online content is a service to both victims and offenders. In the spring of 2016 the European Commission against Racism and Intolerance published an extensive policy recommendation report for the purposes of combating online hate (ECRI, 2016). The report includes an extensive terminology and definition of hate speech, perhaps the most detailed of its kind to date. The purpose of the policy report is to define official boundaries for what actually constitutes online hate speech, and also to provide a kind of manual for member states tackling these issues.

Lately, we have also seen evidence of increasing moderation, or attempted waste management if you will, in particular from news media outlets that have allowed comments and discussion on their platforms. A number of these outlets have either limited or disabled comments and discussion altogether on some of their news stories due to excessive amounts of negative, and in many cases hateful, comments (e.g. Gross, 2014; Kantomaa, 2015; Pullinen, 2015). What makes this interesting is that the highly valued ideology of the free sharing of opinions, ideas and (mis)information online may soon be subject to a more reserved and regulated approach. At what point do the costs of damaging online content outweigh the benefits of uninhibited expression? At what point is it appropriate for legislation to limit rights previously assumed to be necessary and natural? This may have fundamental implications for the future if such restrictive policies become the new norm governing social media expression. Whether this would be an effective solution is another matter. However, as can be noted from a study by Kiesler and colleagues (1984) three decades ago, there has been relatively little progress in regard to online behaviour: "People in computer-mediated groups were more uninhibited than they were in face-to-face groups as measured by uninhibited verbal behaviour, defined as frequency of remarks containing swearing, insults, name calling, and hostile comments" (Kiesler, Siegel & McGuire, 1984, p. 1129).

In the most extreme cases, this reversion to more controlled civility could mean a return from a Web 3.0 to a Web 1.0 type online society, with a limited number of users having power over content production for mass consumption. Now, this seems like an unlikely scenario, given the extent to which various tools for connectivity and online consumption and expression have become intertwined with the daily life of the global population. Given this interplay between high levels of online consumption and the desire to protect users from serious harm through targeted content, the future of social media is sure to be an interesting one. At the moment, Facebook and YouTube, the two most popular social media platforms used by hundreds of millions daily, are also the sites where exposure to hate, and the consequent harm to wellbeing, are most common. Short tweets on the highly popular Twitter can also result in similar consequences for many online users (e.g. Oksanen, Hawdon, Holkeri, Näsi & Räsänen, 2014; see also Chapter 4 above). Therefore, the future policies of social media platforms will have a significant impact on the future culture of online hate, as high levels of use and high levels of harm seem to go hand in hand online. These policies will determine the reasonable limits of discussion in terms of what levels of extremism and forms of expression are acceptable given public health concerns.

Furthermore, the homogenising effect of the Internet can result in reinforcing the early behavioural patterns found most attractive by a particular individual, as like-minded people come together to form various types of personalised bubbles. Together, these may serve to further intensify the polarisation effect by reinforcing social identity bubbles as contrasting opinions are filtered out to facilitate content determined as most likely to match past behaviour. This may result in ever more people moving into smaller and more specific networks where interaction is focused on those who are already familiar to one another and/or share similar ideologies. This limitation on the mixing of opinions, facts, social norms and points of view may encourage harmful behaviours or attitudes.

Depending on control, the role of anonymity may also become less significant. If interactions are limited in terms of content or expression, the role of alternate versions of the self will also evolve. Social media are currently expanding, with services such as Instagram or Periscope and tools for image- and video-sharing becoming increasingly popular. These methods for wide-scale self-presentation through customising how others view the user are growing faster than many prominent social networking sites based on interaction. Rather than being a tool for communication, social media appear to have become more of a tool for developing self-identity through more calculated methods of image building. These new tools offer much more control in terms of what one's identity actually represents. From the perspective of hate, if social media become more visual and less verbal, will the result be more moderate social interaction? Furthermore, wide-scale effects are also influenced by concentrations of high-consumption groups; different demographics tend to use social media for different purposes and consequently group online behavioural characteristics in terms of age, for example, are important factors when considering what platforms or services are most significant in the setting.

In dealing with hate online, information, anonymity and social networks play a highly influential role. The irony is that the same three elements are also at the heart of what makes the Internet great for so many of its users. This brings into focus the often fine line that users tread in terms of whether the positives outweigh the negatives in online interaction, though the positives seem to be winning given the immense user base of various social media platforms. However, certain trends discussed do represent a cause for concern due to the wide-scale potential effect of users targeting others. But how do we prevent damaging content without limiting the numerous benefits that rely on those same avenues of expression?

Looking to the future, a few key areas are worthy of further development. First, online literacy can become a tool for clarifying the online content environment. This involves, first, achieving a better understanding of and distinguishing between information and misinformation, extreme bias and reasonable opinion. Second, an improved understanding of the value of anonymity and its role in privacy rather than as a disguise for deviance may also be helpful in determining who is planning harm and who is simply seeking new avenues for neutral or beneficial expression and exploration. And, third, developing a more complete view of dangerous pockets in social networks and how they are reinforced by the pattern recognition of the online environment can lend itself to more effective methods of meeting identity and expressional needs without nurturing cycles of hate and social harm.

If the risks associated with consumption of the social Internet in terms of widespread negative effects on wellbeing continue to grow, fundamental changes in how we experience the online world may follow. In such a scenario, tighter control of what is allowed online might become the new norm. This would be the very opposite of the original premise that motivated the development of the Internet in the first place. Moving forward in the study of how best to balance widely perceived opportunities and risks that tend to grow together, the key seems to lie in determining how much of a good thing is too much, and why that too much can make the good thing go bad.

References

ECRI (2016). ECRI General policy recommendation No. 15 on combating hate speech. Retrieved from www.coe.int/t/dghl/monitoring/ecri/activities/GPR/EN/Recommendation _N15/REC-15-2016-015-ENG.pdf.

European Commission (2016). European Commission and IT companies announce code of conduct on illegal online hate speech. Retrieved from http://europa.eu/rapid/press-release_IP-16-1937_en.htm.

Gross, D. (2014, 21 November). Online comments are being phased out. *CNN*. Retrieved from http://edition.cnn.com/2014/11/21/tech/web/online-comment-sections/.

Johnson, E. H. (1990). *The Deadly Emotions: The Role of Anger, Hostility, and Aggression in Health and Emotional Well-Being*. Santa Barbara, CA: Praeger Publishers.

Kantomaa, R. (2015, 1 September). MTV Uutiset sulkee osan verkkokeskustelusta – tarkoitus suitsia vihapuheen määrää. *MTV Uutiset*. Retrieved from www.mtv.fi/uutiset/kotimaa/artikkeli/mtv-uutiset-sulkee-osan-verkkokeskustelusta-tarkoitus-suitsia-vihapuheen-maaraa/5290206.

Kiesler, S., Siegel, J., & McGuire, T. W. (1984). Social psychological aspects of computer-mediated communication. *American Psychologist*, *39*(10), 1123–1134. DOI: 10.1037/0003-066X.39.10.1123.

Lapidot-Lefler, N., & Barak, A. (2012). Effects of anonymity, invisibility, and lack of eye-contact on toxic online disinhibition. *Computers in Human Behavior*, *28*(2), 434–443. DOI: 10.1016/j.chb.2011.10.014.

Lea, M., Spears, R., & de Groot, D. (2001). Knowing me, knowing you: Anonymity effects on social identity processes within groups. *Personality and Social Psychology Bulletin*, *27*(5), 526–537. DOI: 10.1177/0146167201275002.

Martin, R. C., Coyier, K. R., VanSistine, L. M., & Schroeder, K. L. (2013). Anger on the Internet: The perceived value of rant-sites. *Cyberpsychology, Behavior, and Social Networking*, *16*(2), 119–122.

Mullin, J. (2012, 2 August). Tim Berners-Lee takes the stand to keep the web free. *Wired*. Retrieved from www.wired.com/2012/02/tim-berners-lee-patent/.

Oksanen, A., Hawdon, J., Holkeri, E., Näsi, M., & Räsänen, P. (2014). Exposure to online hate among young social media users. *Sociological Studies of Children & Youth, 18*, 253–273. DOI: 10.1108/S1537-466120140000018021.

Pullinen, J. (2015, 1 September). Suljemme kommenttiosiomme, koska jotainhan tässä on tehtävä. *Nyt*. Retrieved from http://nyt.fi/a1305981595801.

Putnam, R. D. (1995). Bowling alone: America's declining social capital. *Journal of Democracy*, *6*(1), 65–78.

Suls, J., & Bunde, J. (2005). Anger, anxiety, and depression as risk factors for cardiovascular disease: The problems and implications of overlapping affective dispositions. *Psychological Bulletin, 131*(2), 260–300. DOI: 10.1037/0033-2909.131.2.260.

Sunstein, C. R., & Hastie, R. (2015). *Wiser: Getting Beyond Groupthink to Make Groups Smarter*. Cambridge, MA: Harvard Business Press.

Tajfel, H., & Turner, J. C. (1979). An integrative theory of intergroup conflict. In W. G. Austin & S. Worchel (Eds.), *The Social Psychology of Intergroup Relations* (pp. 33–48). Monterey, CA: Brooks-Cole.

Index

Page numbers in *italics* denote tables, those in **bold** denote figures.